◆◆◆◆◆◆◆◆◆◆◆◆◆◆◆◆◆◆◆◆◆◆◆◆◆◆◆◆◆◆

IMPROVING
COLLEGE TEACHING

◆◆◆◆◆◆◆◆◆◆◆◆◆◆◆◆◆◆◆◆◆◆◆◆◆◆◆◆◆◆

Maryellen Weimer

IMPROVING
COLLEGE TEACHING

Strategies
for Developing
Instructional
Effectiveness

Jossey-Bass Publishers

San Francisco • Oxford • 1990

IMPROVING COLLEGE TEACHING
Strategies for Developing Instructional Effectiveness
by Maryellen Weimer

Copyright © 1990 by: Jossey-Bass Inc., Publishers
350 Sansome Street
San Francisco, California 94104
&
Jossey-Bass Limited
Headington Hill Hall
Oxford OX3 0BW

Library of Congress Cataloging-in-Publication Data

Weimer, Maryellen, date.
    Improving college teaching : strategies for developing
instructional effectiveness / Maryellen Weimer.
        p.   cm. — (The Jossey-Bass higher education series)
    Includes bibliographical references.
    ISBN 1-55542-200-4 (alk. paper)
    1. College teaching.   I. Series.
LB2331.W37   1990
378.1'25 — dc20   89-28865
                                                              CIP

Manufactured in the United States of America

The paper in this book meets the guidelines for
permanence and durability of the Committee on
Production Guidelines for Book Longevity of
the Council on Library Resources.

JACKET DESIGN BY WILLI BAUM

FIRST EDITION

Code 9002

✦ ✦

The Jossey-Bass
Higher Education Series

Consulting Editor
Teaching and Learning

Kenneth E. Eble

CONTENTS

ix

◆ ◆

PREFACE

WHY WRITE a book on better college teaching? Quite simply because it could be improved. Faculty preparation in graduate school continues to offer very little or no instruction on how to teach. Faculty continue to rely on the teaching methods they have always used — this despite research documenting the need for students to learn actively. More often than not the choice of instructional method is a habitual one rather than a reasoned decision based on the instructional objectives of the course and content for the day. Put another way, college teachers teach pretty much as they were taught.

Moreover, levels of instructional quality have not made the dramatic upturn that one might expect as a result of the attention focused on faculty and instructional development during the last twenty years. For the first time, a sizable number of schools have attempted to intervene and improve instructional quality in systematic ways. Some of those attempts have been successful; others have not; still others have yet to be assessed. The movement may be making headway, but the continuing national concern about the classroom experiences of college students lends credence to the conclusion that much work remains to be done.

The need to improve college teaching should not be taken as a sign that college teaching across the continent is in a state of precipitous decline, however. Empirical evidence does not document declining instructional effectiveness. Rather, it seems that much is as it has always been. Instructional methods are the same, faculty preparation has not changed, and instructional development is still not widely offered to faculty. As a result, the nature and quality of college teaching have not changed.

Yet all is not as it has always been. Certain factors make this an especially good time to confront individual faculty members and their institutions with an instructional improvement agenda. To begin with, several credible national reports and recognized educational experts have been critical of higher education, most especially pointing a finger at the quality and conditions of college teaching (Association of American Colleges, 1985; National Institute of Education, 1984; Bowen and Schuster, 1986; Boyer, 1987). For too long, there has been too little emphasis on the effects that classroom experiences have on student decisions to change majors or institutions. These national reports and recently published books have caused the higher education community to take note. Taking the status quo in college teaching for granted is not as easy as it once was.

Still other factors add to the timeliness of this reassessment. Parents, if not students, have responded to the rising costs of a college education with rising levels of "consumerism." Providers of educational "products" are expected to be accountable much like most other producers, and although measuring the relative merit of the product presents some challenges, the current move to assess educational outcomes may soon make educational consumer reports a logical next step.

Moreover, the information explosion is a reality, especially for the beleaguered faculty member who must include more and more "essential" information in a course that has not changed in length. Even fields strongly oriented toward teaching content are now beginning to acknowledge that students need skills that are more enduring than rapidly growing and changing academic content. Students can no longer be taught all that they will need to know throughout a career in the space of a few short years before they start work. Christopher Knapper (1988, p. 1) made this point especially well in an interview about his *Lifelong Learning and Higher Education* (1985, with A. Cropley): "We are advocating the importance of people learning from life and throughout life. Obviously this contrasts markedly [with] our traditional system of 'education by inoculation' in which students are given a sort of preventative dose of fifteen years or so of education in the (false) hope that they will never have to bother with it again."

With the recognition that students need learning skills comes something much harder for college faculty members to acknowledge. They are trained to teach content. Most hope that by virtue of association with an academic discipline, students will learn how people in that field solve problems, generate theories, raise questions, and test answers. Unfortunately, sophisticated learning skills such as these are not easily acquired by osmosis, especially by many students in college today. The learning must be more deliberate, and that makes the teaching more difficult. This changing nature of the instructional task may be the reason traditional teaching methods now seem less effective.

Moreover, the psychologically draining aspects of teaching are only beginning to be recognized. A variety of publications, including *Academic Workplace: New Demands, Heightened Tensions* (Austin and Gamson, 1983) and *Coping with Faculty Stress* (Seldin, 1987), address issues associated with faculty stress and burnout. Keeping teaching fresh and invigorated over a number of years, especially when the teaching assignment basically stays the same, presents formidable challenges to the instructor and institution.

In this book I take all these factors into account as I attempt to show how college teaching can be improved. Researchers (Feldman, 1976, for example) have identified the components of effective instruction, and the good news is that they are not divinely bestowed gifts but acquired skills. Armed with a clearer understanding of what constitutes effective instruction, those charged with instructional improvement can show faculty members how to incorporate the desired components into their own teaching styles in ways that increase their overall effectiveness.

This book takes a practical, no-nonsense approach to improving college teaching but does so recognizing the delicate balance that must be negotiated between individual and institutional efforts. When it comes to implementing changes in the college classroom, only one force is capable of making those changes and that is the faculty member who teaches the class in question. As already intimated, he or she frequently lacks training and also often institutional incentive to motivate the changes. Yet the instructor stands there, "where the rubber meets the road," in a position to make better college teaching a reality.

Institutions and those in them who are concerned about and committed to quality undergraduate education can and should stand behind individual faculty efforts, but how and with what? Institutions cannot send faculty members out on the quest for better teaching unaided, but how do they stimulate and then support those efforts in ways that recognize the professor's centrality to the improvement process? This inherent tension between the efforts of the individual and those of the institution are explored, elaborated, and repeatedly raised in the chapters that follow.

Fortunately, attempts to improve college teaching are not new. Over the last twenty years they have been a central part of the faculty/instructional development movement, and much has been learned about efforts to encourage and support faculty activities in the classroom. Simply stated, these experiences have taught us that there is no one "best" or "right" way to teach in college. All sorts of successful programs and activities have been reported. *Improving College Teaching* is filled with examples. Their effectiveness almost always depends on the match between initiatives and activities, between instructional needs and institutional culture.

Determining what initiatives to match with what culture is not always easy, but the first step for an institution is to learn from what others have tried. What do we know about how improvement works? What motivates a faculty member to participate? How should instructors go about implementing changes? What activities and resources do they need? How do institutions go about incorporating such activities and resources into their structure? What are the organizational options? This book offers answers to those questions — not right answers, but options, which it presents, reviews, and evaluates so that institutions can approach the task with the knowledge and information they need to make informed choices.

At the outset, it is important to clarify the terminology used in this book and its relationship to the language of the faculty/instructional development movement. In spite of noble efforts to clarify definitions in the beginning (Bergquist and Phillips, 1975a; Gaff, 1975), mixed usage and subsequent confusion have arisen (Riegle, 1987). In the literature of the movement, *instructional development* first meant curricular enhancement and changes in the structure, organization, and content of courses, as well as the development of various instructional materials supporting the curricular changes. *Faculty development* started out meaning the enhancement of teaching skill but soon became a more inclusive term connoting a broad range of professional activities, from support for scholarship to counseling on personal problems (for example, chemical dependency) that impinge on professional effectiveness. In the midst of all this, administrators and other well-meaning but uninformed folk, unaware of "official" definitions, started programs and activities at their institutions, and meanings of the terms have become confounded. To clarify, this book is about improving college teaching, that is, the performance of faculty members in the classroom. Throughout the book this is referred to as *instructional development*.

Audience

The book is for anyone responsible for or concerned about instructional quality within a postsecondary institution. Specifically, it is for instructional developers, new and old—and is aimed at refining their approach, to increase their impact on the instruction of the faculty members with whom they deal; it is for academic leaders, department heads, deans, division chairpersons, academic vice-presidents, and provosts—and is aimed at increasing their understanding of and role in the improvement of college teaching; it is for faculty committees, task forces, and ad hoc groups charged with assessing the instructional climate at their institution and making recommendations about improving it. And the book is written for individuals (be they an isolated department head or a concerned faculty member in a large department) who may not have much in the way of resources or training but believe instruction at their institution needs to be improved and want to do something to make it better.

However, *Improving College Teaching* is not for faculty members per se; that is, it is not the volume to give to an instructor who "needs" to improve. Instead, it focuses on the improvement process, particularly on how institutions and individuals in institutions can implement and direct improvement activities. The individual faculty member who wants to teach better may be helped by that information but not as directly as by information on teaching techniques and strategies.

Overview of the Contents

The book is organized in three major parts. The first part places the improvement process in a context. In Chapter One I look at the higher education environment and explain why improving college teaching is no simple task. Sizable impediments stand in the way, even at colleges and universities where the agenda is fully endorsed and supported, to say nothing of those places where individuals may labor against a strong institutional bias in favor of research. Nevertheless, faculty participation in improvement efforts can be cultivated, and in Chapter Two I suggest approaches that encourage such involvement. In Chapter Three I propose a five-step improvement process for approaching better teaching in a systematic, deliberate, and thoughtful way.

The second part of the book is devoted to an exploration of the activities that can be used in the improvement process. I consider the role of instructional evaluation in the process (Chapter Four), spotlighting the activities involved in such evaluation so that they are seen as something other than collecting a few general impressions of the teaching by way of a bureaucratically efficient, machine-scorable short form. The discussion of student evaluation results focuses on translating those results into teaching improvements. Chapter Five presents a wide variety of activities designed to acquire information about the teaching. These include reading programs, course material reviews, seminars, and videotaped teaching samples. Chapter Six explores the role of colleagues in mutual improvement activities. Chapter Seven focuses on the role of an institution's academic leaders in creating a climate conducive to improvement and includes concrete suggestions.

Part Three focuses on institutional options. Chapter Eight presents an overview of possibilities, including improvement efforts that are centered on individuals, on committees, and on programs. This chapter also attempts to identify the strengths and weaknesses associated with each option and illustrates how the options can be matched to the institution. Chapter Nine profiles eleven programs that show how institutionally specific structures evolve out of general options and can be made to fit the culture of the institution and its faculty. This chapter concludes by offering advice to institutions or individuals who are about to embark on improvement efforts within an institution. The final chapter, Chapter Ten, reiterates and reemphasizes the themes of the book.

That the objectives of this book and what it proposes are ambitious cannot be denied. College teaching has in the past (even the recent past) remained relatively impervious to attempts to change it, relatively unresponsive to stinging but legitimate criticisms. Yet I embark on this ambitious agenda optimistically. More is known about college teaching than ever before, and that includes research on how it can and should be improved. Faculty do not want to teach poorly. Even those embittered by the neglect of teaching and those infatuated with research emphases know that knowledge must be shared. Learning can be an independent activity, but instructors realize that unshared wisdom has little enduring value. To share knowledge is to teach, and to share knowledge effectively is to guarantee the preservation and elaboration of what most faculty have labored long to learn.

There is something else most faculty know but may have trouble admitting. Books and now data bases pass along the facts, but teachers inspire the passion. Some faculty members falter there, dubious of that role, but when the student begins to understand as the teacher labors to explain, most teachers find themselves willing participants in the teaching-learning process — eager to do whatever might be required to make it more effective. Peter Drucker (1985, p. 192) explains why this is so and justifies an optimistic beginning: "The smile of learning on the student's face is more addictive than any drug or narcotic."

Acknowledgments

For some time, I felt a need for a book on instructional improvement at the postsecondary level. Fortunately, Gale Erlandson at Jossey-Bass recognized the same need, and we were able to share our visions of what those wishing to improve college teaching might benefit from knowing. From the beginning, Gale has contributed to this project immeasurably. Kenneth E. Eble agreed to serve as consulting editor and helped significantly until his sudden and untimely death. His detailed, insightful, and sometimes acerbic comments gave focus and direction to revisions of the first seven chapters. His letters to a worried first-time author are now treasured possessions to be savored, smiled over, and greatly appreciated. College teaching has lost one of its most articulate and ardent spokespersons.

Thanks are due to others as well. Christopher Knapper and Eugene Melander reviewed and offered suggestions on the first three chapters. As I wrote, James Rhem looked over my shoulder, urging me to say it clearly and pointing out passive verbs that needed to be active. Ann Rigo typed, revised, and printed the manuscript many, many times. Michael (my favorite person) and Fluffy (my favorite pet) reminded me that even authors of "important" books must take time to love and be loved.

State College, Pennsylvania   Maryellen Weimer
November 1989

◆ ◆

THE AUTHOR

MARYELLEN WEIMER is director of instructional development at the Pennsylvania State University. She received her B.A. degree (1970) from Seattle Pacific University in speech, her M.A. degree (1972) from the University of Oregon in rhetoric and public address, and her Ph.D. degree (1981) from the Pennsylvania State University in speech communications. Before assuming her current position at the Pennsylvania State University, she was assistant professor of speech communications at Linfield College in McMinnville, Oregon.

Weimer's scholarly interests focus on college teaching and the process of improving it, particularly at large, research-oriented institutions. She is the editor of an issue of Jossey-Bass's New Directions for Teaching and Learning series, entitled *Teaching Large Courses Well* (1987), and coauthor of *How Am I Teaching? Forms and Activities for Acquiring Instructional Input* (1988, with M. Kerns and J. Parrett). She has published extensively in *College Teaching* and in 1987 began editing *The Teaching Professor,* a monthly newsletter on teaching with eighteen thousand faculty subscribers. She regularly serves as a consultant to colleges and universities across the country on instructional improvement issues.

To my aunt, Ellen P. Bump,
who lent me books, bought me books,
and taught me to love books.

◆◆◆◆◆◆◆◆◆◆◆◆◆◆◆◆◆◆◆◆◆◆◆◆◆◆◆◆◆

PART ONE

REMOVING BARRIERS TO TEACHING IMPROVEMENT

1

◆◆◆◆◆◆◆◆◆◆◆◆◆◆◆◆◆◆◆◆◆◆◆◆◆◆◆◆◆◆◆

What Makes
the Improvement
of College Teaching
Difficult?

DESPITE the fact college teaching needs improvement and empirical evidence shows how its effectiveness can be increased, despite the readily available experience of college teachers who have improved, and despite the fact that the academic community is attending to calls for better teaching, the teaching practices of college faculty members are not easily changed. And so even though the time is right and the chances of success are real, this will be no easy victory. Those committed to better college teaching must start the task fully aware of what lies ahead.

Formidable barriers stand in the way of teaching improvement. First, there are faculty attitudes — often rigidly held assumptions and beliefs about teaching and learning that are resistant to change. Second, certain characteristics of the academic profession as a whole impede the process. Finally, certain conditions prevalent at postsecondary institutions throughout North America affect the academic environment in ways that hinder — if not militate against — increased instructional effectiveness. Taken together, these faculty attitudes, orientations of the profession, and institutional environments add up to serious motivational problems and outright resistance to improvement initiatives.

Faculty Assumptions

Faculty make a number of flawed assumptions about teaching and learning. Unfortunately, these seemingly obvious truisms seriously inhibit both individual and institutional efforts to do something about instructional quality. Consider three such assumptions.

If you know it, you can teach it. Graduate school curriculums in the main are rigorous, designed with one objective in mind: developing the skills of scholarship. As the president of the Council of Graduate Schools in the United States (LaPidus, 1987, p. 4) recently wrote, "It remains true that Ph.D. education in this country, at least in the arts and sciences, is based on the concept of turning out scholars capable of doing independent work and not on the idea of training college teachers." It is assumed that these terminal degrees qualify recipients to teach. In other words, designers and overseers of graduate curriculums (most often senior faculty at the institutions), see nothing in *teaching* that graduate students need to "study" in a formal, educational sense.

The importance of content competence in instructional effectiveness cannot be denied. "Knowledge of content" appears frequently on research-generated lists of characteristics of effective college teachers (Feldman, 1976). The problem is not the importance given to this qualification of college teachers. Rather, it is the assumption that this is the *only* qualification, the single ingredient of effective instruction. Empirical inquiries into the nature of effective instruction repeatedly result in lists of characteristics or dimensions. One such list, based on an assessment of a large collection of studies, appears in Sherman and others (1987) and includes enthusiasm, clarity, preparation and organization, stimulation (of interest and thinking), and knowledge (and love) of the content. To know the content is not enough. In fact, some studies suggest that certain other characteristics, such as instructor enthusiasm and involvement in the content, may be more important than the factual knowledge of it (Musella and Rusch, 1968).

If the teaching is not going well and faculty assume that "if you know it, you can teach it," they are forced to conclude that their knowledge of the content is inadequate. Gaff (1978, p. 61) surveyed 1,642 college students, asking them to rate, in terms of how much they were needed, a list of thirty possible ways college teaching could be improved. Improving the content competence of instructors was rated last on the list. Even those college teachers who find these student ratings suspect are not likely to quarrel with the conclusion. In the vast majority of situations, faculty know their course materials. What frustrates them is their apparent inability to communicate their knowledge to students.

And then there are those legendary full professors who do know the content, who get books and articles published and do research and receive grants, but whose course enrollments remain consistently low and dropout rates are legendary. Without question they know the content, but can they teach it? More important, if they learn more, will they teach better?

Finally, the equating of content mastery with instructional effectiveness inhibits instructional improvement because it makes teaching an activity without form or substance in its own right. This simple, reductionist view of teaching is not only unfortunate, it is naive. The research efforts of the recent and not so recent past have clarified much about teaching, but by no means all. The highly dynamic and idiosyncratic functions of this phenomenon make it very difficult to predict outcomes and explain variable interactions. Moreover, what the research says in its formal and technical way, any teacher can tell you in far more experiential terms. Some days in class, nothing comes together; on other memorable occasions, the connection between teacher, student, and content happens and the whole classroom lights up. To believe that if you know it, you can teach it is to have a vision of teaching that is narrow and simplistic, a blind spot that makes instructional problems unrelated to content much more difficult to discern.

Good teachers are born. A second frequent faculty assumption is that good teachers are born, not made. Many college teachers still equate good teaching with a gift bestowed by some divinity. If you have "received" it, you have been blessed; if not, well, you must make do and not be bitter.

Certainly one of the reasons faculty members are attracted to such a dubious proposition is the high degree of variability in teaching styles. Effective instructors use widely different techniques and strategies. Some "perform" in very theatrical ways;

others are intense, maybe even intimidating, as they scrutinize students for signs of seriousness and dedication. Some use humor; others rarely crack a smile and avoid small talk. Looking at such a hodgepodge of approaches, it is difficult to see common characteristics and therefore easy to equate teaching gifts with birthrights.

The answer, however, is just not that simple, and faculty denied the birthright should not be excused so forthrightly. Granted, individual teaching styles vary widely, but research since the 1930s has inquired into the components of effective instruction and keeps generating lists containing the same characteristics (Sherman and others, 1987). The problem is that the characteristics are abstract and can be incorporated into an individual's teaching style with many subtle and idiosyncratic variations. Take, for example, one frequently identified characteristic of effective instruction, enthusiasm. Good teachers get involved with their subject matter and attack teaching tasks with energy, zest, and obvious concern.

Enthusiasm is an abstraction. It lacks tangible form and substance. Its presence (or absence) is conveyed by behaviors that have come to be associated with it. This is where the variation in individual style emerges. There are many, many behaviors in isolation and in combination that convey enthusiasm. Some instructors communicate their enthusiasm through vigorous physical delivery. They gesture, run to the chalkboard, point to the diagram, and walk out to the students. Their movements are filled with purpose and energy. Other instructors convey enthusiasm with intensity. Ensconced firmly behind the podium, faces serious, they share content relentlessly. Their eye contact is direct and compelling and never wavers. Their delivery fits the seriousness and complexity of the content. Still others convey messages of enthusiasm with vocal variety. The pitch rises and falls, the volume and speed change. When the point is important the tone rises, the pace quickens, and the volume increases. Already it is obvious that potential variations on the enthusiasm theme are limitless — and enthusiasm is only one of many characteristics of effective instruction.

Research has done a good job of identifying the general

elements of effective instruction. It has done less well clarifying their relationship to each other. For example, which ones are most important? What if one is missing from an instructor's teaching? Will the presence of the others compensate? Given the variation in effective teaching styles, one suspects the characteristics interact with each other in very different ways. This makes an understanding and description of good teaching complicated—but not impossible.

Instructors who equate good teaching with divine gifts need first to be confronted with the research-identified characteristics of effective instruction. When faced with that list (a good set of sample lists appears in table form in Miller, 1975, pp. 32–33), they readily acknowledge that it contains few surprises. This helps to demystify the aura of the unknown that surrounds good teaching. Equally obvious when faculty view the list is the fact that the components of effective instruction look much more like acquirable skills than divine gifts. Faculty members can learn to convey enthusiasm more effectively. They can cultivate organizational skills. In fact, most already have, at least to some degree, and will even so acknowledge when asked to compare how they teach now (five, ten, fifteen years into their careers) with their first experiences in the college classroom. Most are quick to point out that they learned from the school of hard knocks, but even so, on their own they learned some tricks that made life in the classroom easier for them and their students. Most teach more effectively now than they did then. That, albeit haphazard, development of skills opens the door to the possibility that good teachers are not just born, but can be made as well.

Faculty teach content. The third assumption that hinders efforts to improve is the strong faculty orientation to teach content. This they see as their mission; to teach physics, chemistry, anthropology, economics, or whatever the discipline. The problem is that sometimes their allegiance to the content is much stronger than their loyalty to students. This explains why some faculty members end up teaching *content* but not necessarily *students*. The orientation toward content is understandable given the focus of graduate school curriculums. However, faculty allegiance to content makes efforts to improve college teaching difficult. As information continues to grow at an explosive rate, there continues to be more and more content to teach. Faculty feel pressure to teach more, but their courses have not been correspondingly lengthened. This circumstance is even more troublesome to students, especially those entering college insufficiently prepared or after a lengthy hiatus away from formal educational experiences.

It is very difficult to persuade college teachers to relinquish their hold on the content. After all, most professors aspire to a reputation for rigor, high academic standards, and "toughness." Such a reputation can be acquired by teaching courses that contain plenty of complicated content. The news many faculty members have missed is that content changes — and especially rapidly these days, although Alfred North Whitehead made the same point much earlier: "Knowledge doesn't keep any better than fish." Some have attempted to calculate the extent of content change. On the basis of the rate at which scientific knowledge doubles, one chemist (Lagowski, 1985) suggests that 80 percent of the knowledge a chemist will need during a thirty-five-year span will be acquired following completion of formal education.

Faculty need to teach students how to think critically, how to analyze, synthesize, and evaluate information, how to question, and how to articulate ideas clearly and collaborate with others. And faculty readily espouse these educational objectives. Seventy-eight percent of the respondents in a survey by Gaff (1978, p. 55) attached "great importance to the teaching of critical thinking." In a corresponding survey of students, Gaff reports that only 28 percent said faculty spent time in class developing these skills. What college teachers seem to assume is that by virtue of being in the presence of a particular brand of academic content, students will learn how to think, problem solve, critically assess, and so on. Unfortunately, that does not happen as effectively or efficiently as when faculty members use the content to teach those skills directly.

In spite of the improperness of this content orientation, faculty deserve a certain benevolence and understanding. How does one teach a student to think? What teaching techniques and classroom activities will achieve that objective? The answers are neither easy nor obvious. Teaching content, with its straightforward delineation of facts and details, its establishment of principles and propositions, is easier by comparison. Giving a student a list to memorize taxes teachers much less than trying to explain why the items belong on the list and how so categorizing the content reveals underlying principles. Yet if we are to improve instruction, we must tackle the faculty propensity to teach only content. These objectives will only be obtained when faculty cease to view content as the sole aim of education and start seeing it as the means by which much larger objectives are accomplished.

All three of the foregoing assumptions, frequently expressed in faculty dialogue and often reflected in teaching techniques, offer challenges to those committed to better college teaching. Unfortunately, they are not the only factors contributing to those challenges.

Professional Characteristics

As members of a profession governed by shared values and ethical orientations, faculty members approach teaching tasks similarly. They share a common understanding of the expectations and responsibilities belonging to college teachers and perform accordingly. Unfortunately, their collected lore on college teaching does not jibe with what is known about effective instruction and how students learn. As a result, improvement agendas are much more difficult to implement. Consider three ways in which the profession itself stands in the way of better college teaching.

The college teaching profession does not recognize the need for instructional training. A substantial number of Ph.D.'s today start jobs in colleges and universities never having taught before and never having any formal instruction in how to teach. This is no new professional fact of life. The large majority of veteran faculty members, though able to produce transcripts documenting course work in virtually every aspect of their content specialty, cannot point to one class that addressed instructional issues.

The problem with faculty members who are untrained to teach is that they teach generally unaware of how they do it. This results in their inability to account for *why* they do it that way. In other words, they lack instructional awareness. This lack of instructional awareness accounts for well-educated, intelligent, and respected professionals being dubbed with unflattering nicknames by students who count the number of times a pet phrase or favorite gesture is repeated during a given class period. It also explains a lack of variety in instructional strategy and an inability to cope in a classroom when things do not go as expected.

It is unlikely that the profession can be persuaded outright that college teachers need to be trained. It is even more unlikely that current college teachers will return to graduate school for the missing course work. The task, then, for the would-be improver of college teaching is on-the-job training designed to make faculty members aware of how they do teach and how they could teach. However, even before the training, college teachers must be convinced that there is something of value to learn about instruction. If a faculty member has taught without training and been reasonably successful for the last twenty years, even this recognition may require sizable persuasive efforts.

Nevertheless, faculty members can be persuaded if they understand that a clear sense of how they teach — what teaching strategies they use and what assumptions about teaching and learning underlie the choices they have made — puts them in a much better position to expand their instructional repertoire. Understanding how they seek to accomplish the instructional objectives they have chosen enables them to consider and assess alternatives for achieving those same objectives. Knowing the proclivities of a teaching style enables a faculty member to make better decisions about alternatives. Not every method of conveying enthusiasm works equally well for every faculty member. Instructional awareness means that choices about alternatives are more likely to be informed, and that realization gives college teachers a better chance of improving instructional effectiveness.

Stemming from this first professional characteristic is a second, closely related one: *The profession is only beginning to under-*

stand that teaching across a number of years is psychologically and emo-tionally draining. This understanding came when institutions stopped adding faculty positions (in 1980 the Carnegie Council on Policy Studies in Higher Education, p. 305, reported net additions were hovering at 0 percent) and when faculty movement between institutions declined from 8 percent in the mid 1960s to 1 percent in 1982 (Chait and Ford, 1982, p. 7). For the first time, faculty members and their institutions confronted the fact that their relationships might indeed be long-term ones. Perhaps this explains why almost 30 percent of one faculty study group reported feeling trapped in their current positions (Carnegie Foundation for the Advancement of Teaching, 1985). For those faculty members who do not feel trapped, new legislation prohibiting mandatory retirement may well make institutions feel that they are the ones who are trapped.

As for the psychological and emotional drain, it happens this way. For the faculty member who spends any length of time at a given institution, teaching assignments tend to settle into a more or less steady diet of the same course year after year. Faculty members within a department are encouraged to develop specialties, and along with them comes a sense of territory. Fairly soon History 351 is Fred's course, and anybody else who wants to teach it is after Fred's "place" (and probably power) in the department.

The implications for instructional improvement lie in the challenges of keeping teaching fresh and invigorated across a number of years while the teaching assignment stays the same. Courses can become comfortable ruts in which the same lectures, texts, assignments, and exams are recycled ad infinitum and sometimes ad nauseum. Teaching becomes a habituated response, conditioned and automatic. The instructor is bored and the students quickly follow suit.

Although bored, instructors who have taught the same course the same way for many years have found for themselves safe, comfortable routines, places where they can ignore or repress the psychologically and emotionally draining aspects of teaching. This results from a sort of nothing-ventured-nothing-lost teaching philosophy, and nothing in the "professional" sense discourages teachers from adopting it. Thus, it is sometimes difficult to get faculty out of safe ruts. To begin, any change of instructional method or content requires work. The old lectures may need to be replaced, old assignments discarded in favor of new ones. Although some faculty who routinely recycle instructional materials will object to the extra work, many more will withdraw from but not admit to the vulnerabilities change implies. Most are used to being in control in the classroom. They have heard all the student questions before and know the answers by heart. New configurations of content will call forth new questions, and what, dear God, if the answer to one of them is not known?

Still, the profession is beginning to recognize the reality of teacher burnout, and that is cause for optimism. However, recognizing that something is a problem and doing something about it are two separate acts. At this point, the task of persuading faculty members to abandon safe but tired teaching techniques falls primarily to those advocating better teaching.

A third professional characteristic is that *the college teaching profession has yet to cope with the implications of changing student populations.* Initially, the profession worried that there would be fewer students. When that did not come to pass except at a few kinds of institutions, the profession took to complaining that college students today are not what they once were. College students have changed and in some profoundly significant ways. Today there are more college students over twenty-five years of age. These students bring to college a rich history of personal experience. They also frequently combine college course work with many other responsibilities, including jobs and family. Some students in college today are not as well prepared as they should be. They may have attended high schools that did not emphasize college preparation. Some students may represent minority groups accessing higher education for the first time. Whatever the reason, they come minus such skills as listening, note taking, reading, and writing, skills that are essential for success in college and that faculty assume students in their courses already have well in hand. Other students enrolled today come without a commitment to college and with little understanding of a college education. They are in school to be trained, to be certified in the profession of their choosing; and they are single-minded in their objective and purpose.

Such a diverse student population is difficult to teach for two reasons. First, what if some of each variety end up in the same class? To whom should the teacher direct the instruction? How does an instructor meet all the instructional needs represented in a given class?

Second, distinctions like the ones mentioned make these students more difficult to teach, because many of the old tried and true techniques do not produce the desired learning outcomes. Faculty members who lack training, who teach pretty much as they always have, tend to be unaware of alternative techniques and strategies better suited to the needs of more diverse populations. With bright, inquisitive students committed to a college education, how the faculty member teaches is less critical. But when students other than the brightest and the best, other than those most highly motivated, end up in college classrooms, their ability to succeed is much more closely tied to how the faculty member conducts the class. With the profession doing little more than complaining about these changing student populations, faculty difficulties in the classroom are deepened.

These three professional characteristics that stand in the way of efforts to improve college teaching seem to coalesce around a declining sense of professionalism about college teaching. The vision of what it means to be a college teacher, what responsibility that imposes in regard to one's students and one's institution seems less sharp — especially among younger faculty members. Among that group, membership in professional organizations such as the American Association of University Professors (AAUP) has declined. Apathy toward university governance prevails on many campuses, and perhaps most indicative of all, the recent reports critical of higher education have come from outside. It is as if the profession never bothered to notice that there is a problem. It is much easier to motivate efforts to improve when there is a sense of pride and vigor about one's profession. In its absence, people wishing to improve college teaching have a much more difficult assignment.

Academic Environments

Two conditions prevailing at most institutions today also add to the difficulties of improving college teaching. First, *most colleges and universities today are having to cope with declining sources of revenue.* Money is not as prevalent as it once was in higher education, and that fact has a number of instructional implications.

For starters, faculty will uniformly complain that instructional facilities are in a state of decline. State-of-the-art classrooms on most campuses today are "art" as it was "stated" twenty years ago. Often classrooms are not cleaned as regularly as they once were. So upon arriving for first period, college teachers and students face classroom litter accumulated from the day or days before. It is hard to take pride in one's teaching and perform consistently well in environments where messages of neglect are so eloquently stated.

Furthermore, if corners must be cut in the instructional budget, one good way to do that is by using more part-time, adjunct professors and/or teaching assistants. With part-time, adjunct professors, the issue is not one of qualifications. The overabundance of Ph.D.'s in many fields has resulted in extraordinarily well-qualified people filling these less than desirable academic positions. The difficulty is for those wishing to support the instructional efforts of these "itinerant" faculty members — many of whom have positions at more than one institution. Most do not have offices on campus and cannot easily attend activities during regular academic hours.

With TAs, the fundamental issue is an old one. These are the most inexperienced of all teachers. But with the attitude toward content that prevails, graduate schools are not predisposed to adding required courses on college teaching. In a time of diminished resources, even training for TAs has few economic incentives. A "trained" TA will teach for two or maybe three years for a department and then be off to another institution, leaving the department with a training investment to make all over again. Moreover, short-term, economically viable training has had declining positive effects in light of the increased numbers of international TAs, who need far more comprehensive orientations to college teaching in our culture.

Next, although few departments and institutions will publicly acknowledge use of this strategy, one good way to trim instructional budgets is by increasing class size. Although there is some evidence that students learn as much in large classes as in smaller ones, students do not like them as well (McKeachie, 1986, p. 181). More important to those wishing to positively effect instructional quality is the fact that faculty find large classes particularly challenging and unpleasant. They tax faculty presentation skills, preclude the possibility of developing personal relationships with students, and prevent teachers from providing more than very modest amounts of feedback.

Finally, declining revenues mean fewer dollars to devote to instructional improvement resources and services. Although improvement initiatives must be under the aegis and control of the faculty member involved, he or she should not be forced to set out on the quest for better teaching unaided. The endeavor deserves support. Yet after the novelty of faculty development wore off and the soft monies to inaugurate activities were expended, many universities failed to replenish the coffers. A number of prestigious centers for instructional enhancement and teaching excellence closed; many of those still in operation sustained major budget cuts (Gustafson and Bratton, 1984); and among those more recently initiated are examples of operations severely understaffed and underfunded. However, an interest in centrally administered instructional development programs and activities seems to be reviving. Membership in the Professional and Organizational Development Network (POD), a national association concerned with faculty and instructional development issues, has more than doubled in the last ten years (M. Svinicki, letter to the author, Jan. 8, 1988). Perhaps colleges are beginning to realize that they must be willing to pay for good teaching with more than lip service.

The second condition inhibiting instructional development at colleges and universities is *higher education's continuing infatuation with the research model.* If one were to inquire of colleges and universities of all sizes and types, "What do you want to be when you grow up?" the most likely answer would be, "A major (if not a top ten) research university." The example may border on hyperbole. Some colleges and universities do realize that objective is not obtainable for them, but they still reinforce the model by valuing and rewarding the research productivity of their faculty, by hiring grant writers who help faculty members develop research proposals, and by generally extolling the virtues of expanded fields of knowledge. That institutions have a role in pushing back the horizons of knowledge is unquestionable. That college teachers have an obligation to keep abreast of and involved in their discipline is equally unarguable. Yet always to value research above teaching is unfair — especially to the millions of students who come to college not to learn how to be researchers but because they need lifelong learning skills. This is not a matter of either/or — the need is for both/and. Until higher education recognizes the inherent value and equality of both its missions, faculty involvement in instructional improvement will never be what it could be. For faculty stuck after thirteen years of teaching in assistant professor ranks because they have not published, the question "Why do anything about teaching?" is both real and legitimate.

Faculty Resistance to Instructional Improvement Efforts

To summarize, the foregoing faculty assumptions, the professional orientations, and the environments at their institutions define for those interested in better college teaching their first task: encouraging faculty participation in improvement efforts. What is there about teaching effectiveness to learn? What professional or institutional recognition comes to those pursuing excellence in the classroom?

Unfortunately, the problem, as early instructional developers discovered, is even more serious than simply a matter of missing motivation. Many faculty members respond to attempts to encourage them to better teaching with open resistance. As Gaff observed in 1978 (p. 47), "Anyone embarking on the road to teaching improvement should anticipate resistance not only from his colleagues and his institutions, but from his fellow reformers and himself as well." In other words, what the instructional developer, department head, or administrator proposes is fine for TAs, ought to be something done for new faculty members, is even okay for those departments that need it, but do not expect *me* to get involved.

What is it about instructional improvement that brings out this overtly negative faculty reaction? Quite simply, faculty feel threatened when attention is directed toward their teaching. Whether or not that response is legitimate, it occurs and must be responded to if efforts to improve teaching are to get off the ground.

Faculty feel threatened for several reasons. First, the need to improve implies incompetence in professional arenas where they see themselves as experts. Most are content specialists — knowledgeable authorities, used to being consulted for answers, advice, and counsel. They are the ones called on to pinpoint the problems and solutions. Moreover, most have taught for many years without being so confronted. They have taught a variety of courses and hundreds of students. They take their teaching for granted. Attention directed toward it catches them off guard, makes them wary and a tad uncomfortable. Could it be they have been doing something "wrong" or "stupid" or "foolish" and doing it in public for all these years?

Faculty are also threatened because teaching requires personal involvement. It cannot occur without instructors communicating something about themselves. When teachers dispense content, they reveal their understanding of that material, their sense of how it is configured and prioritized. When teachers interact with students, the exchanges illustrate how teachers feel about and conduct relationships. When teachers make decisions about course policies and practices, they reveal something about their sense of fairness and justice. When teachers evaluate students, they show how and why they make judgments.

All these revelations make the teacher vulnerable. Maybe the teacher's words and deeds contradict each other and students point that out publicly. Maybe the values the teacher takes pride in upholding, the students choose to challenge — to question and debate. Self-discovery under such circumstances can be painful. It is no wonder that many teachers seek to protect themselves from such encounters. They teach firmly ensconced behind the podium, paying close attention to their detailed lecture notes, and focused exclusively and relentlessly on *all* the content that they must teach. They simply cannot take time to answer questions or discuss the exam or respond to student concerns.

College teaching is unlikely to be improved unless teachers take a good hard look at instructional policies and practices — and give students and colleagues the opportunity to do the same. That magnifies the vulnerabilities just discussed as does the position of teachers in the classroom. Teachers occupy positions of power in the classroom. They are supposed to know, to be the learned experts, to manage the classroom, to be the role models. And they are supposed to be and do all these things in a public arena, the classroom. If they do not or have not and find that out, from their position of power, they have far to fall.

Finally, sometimes faculty greet efforts to improve their teaching reluctantly because their previous experiences in efforts to improve have not been positive. Much of the blame for negative experiences can be attributed to current activities associated with student evaluations. Typically, these evaluations are completed as part of a personnel decision-making process. For faculty members so evaluated, their longevity and quality of life within the academic community are at stake. Because many college teachers are not particularly aware of how they teach and what effect their instructional policies and practices have on students, the evaluation results can sometimes be a surprise. Then, too, there are the poorly designed instruments that may encourage an inaccurate understanding of one's instructional effectiveness by producing bogus data. Some universities make matters worse by disseminating results in ways especially effective in making faculty defensive and hostile.

The nature of the evaluation data complicates the problem still further. The items tend to describe teaching with a few global and abstract phrases. The results give faculty a broad, general sense of their instructional effectiveness. But the results do not focus on details, and the faculty members with low scores and administrative pressure to do something about them are not likely to find answers in data that compare them to others at the same institution. Chapter Four looks more deeply into the role of student evaluations in the improvement process, but early on it must be recognized that some faculty resistance may be attributed to prior experiences with student evaluation.

After reviewing the reasons for faculty resistance to instructional improvement overtures, it is easier to understand (if not accept). However, faculty members themselves have difficulty acknowledging the personal anxiety they feel. To the people who propose improvement activities college teachers may respond that they do not have the time; they will not be teaching this course again until fall; they need to get a particular research project underway; their teaching problems are caused by the kinds of students the institution admits these days; they have already tried the changes being proposed and students do not like them. In other words, college teachers resist efforts to encourage their involvement for all sorts of reasons other than the real ones.

When it comes to admitting fears to themselves and others, faculty members are probably no different from any other group of humans. Admitting fear implies weakness, and our society makes admitting weakness difficult. However, for those who must respond to and overcome faculty apathy and resistance, understanding what may lie behind faculty responses helps to show why some strategies (such as those proposed in Chapter Two) may be more effective than others.

Conclusion

The challenges that face those committed to better college teaching have been explored. Licata (1986, p. 4) asks the hard question: "In the face of an aging, immobile faculty, shifting enrollment trends, declining budgets, spiraling costs, and external calls for accountability and self-regulations, what options promote institutional flexibility and foster faculty vitality and renewal?" This book attempts to identify those options. It does so resting firmly on the premise that college teaching *can* be improved, even at large research universities, even at financially strapped smaller institutions. It can be improved through formal instructional development programs, with less formal ad hoc committees, and by individual faculty members and administrators who care about the experiences students have in classrooms across their campuses. To make that assumption unaware of the impediments that stand in the way, however, would be to embark on a trip with no sense that the road to the final destination is long and hard.

2

❖❖❖❖❖❖❖❖❖❖❖❖❖❖❖❖❖❖❖❖❖❖❖❖❖❖❖

Overcoming
Faculty Resistance
and Encouraging
Participation

SIZABLE barriers stand in the way of better teaching. The rest of this book proposes ways and means around and over them. Any instructional improvement effort must begin with the issue of faculty participation. As things stand, most faculty members are not motivated to improve their teaching. For reasons identified in Chapter One, some even resist the effort. How do we get them involved, especially in light of the barriers?

Begin by considering the question of faculty motivation. We can think of motivation as a force that energizes behavior. The force may be external, hence extrinsic motivation, or it may be internal, intrinsic motivation. With extrinsic motivation there is often no choice — one does something because one has to, not because one wants to. Students study because the instructor has scheduled an exam. Instructors would like students to study because they are interested and want to learn, but most instructors do schedule exams. Some even resort to unannounced quizzes as "forces" necessary to energize the desired behavior.

Those who confront faculty with an instructional improvement agenda face the same sort of dilemma — only the extrinsic motivators here are even less appropriate than they are with students. To "require" faculty to improve their instruction is not much of an option if they have tenure. It is not very realistic given the climates and cultures of most of our institutions. Furthermore, it would not be desirable even if it could be done. What happens in courses where instructors rely heavily on extrinsic motivators? Yes, external forces do "motivate" students to study the material, but only for the duration of the course and rarely thereafter. Students leave the course with bad attitudes and retain little of the information. To "require" faculty to improve their instruction is likely to engender the same poor attitudes and lack of long-term results.

When the motivation to improve is intrinsic, the results are very different. The effects on instruction are more enduring, faculty attitudes are more positive, and faculty commitments to continued improvement are stronger.

When the motivation to improve must come from within the faculty member, the instructional improver occupies an interesting position, one that merits further exploration. At first, it appears to be a difficult and powerless role. But is it? Are there no strategies that one can take that have the potential to energize faculty members? Approaches that encourage their participation in improvement initiatives and activities? Tactics that help to overcome resistance? Consider four.

Approaching Better Teaching as Something for Everyone

Improvement initiatives should not be based on premises of remediation and deficiency with activities targeted only for those who need them. Yes, national reports have documented troublesome aspects of college teaching. Yet it is difficult to say for sure that college teaching is worse now than it was in the past, and to use that as the motivating force behind an improvement effort is to increase automatically the threat to faculty.

Taking this approach does put instructional improvers between the proverbial rock and hard place. On the one hand, they would not be arguing for instructional improvement if there were not some need. Visits to even a few college classrooms verify that the need does exist. On the other hand, if the instructional improver starts talking to and about individual teachers who "need" to improve, efforts to better teaching at an institution will never get off the ground. The way out of this dilemma is to acknowledge the need to improve generally, not in terms of specific individuals.

Administrators should leave the issue of who needs it alone as well. One of the most frequent criticisms leveled against offices and individuals attempting to improve instructional quality on a campus is "You're only helping the faculty members who don't need it." Obviously, administrators are interested in doing something about notoriously bad teachers, but those same administrators must be patient and realize that they may have had a hand in creating the problem vis-a-vis ineffective evaluation and reward systems. These are the most difficult cases and can probably be tackled successfully only after improvement activities are well established and accepted on a campus. The faculty members who need help are frequently the ones with the most to lose. They are not going to be first to request it, and if forced, they are least likely to be helped.

Besides, to some degree the argument of who needs to improve and who does not is bogus. Instructional improvement is for everyone. Granted, different levels of teaching effectiveness exist on campuses. Some teachers do need to improve more than others, but everyone can benefit, including average and excellent teachers. Teaching is very much like running, writing, swimming, painting, and a host of other activities. With practice and attention to detail, performance improves. Even outstanding athletes devote a great deal of time to practice, working to refine already highly effective skills. All faculty members can improve; most should.

This approach encourages faculty participation for several reasons. First, when faculty members see good teachers working to be better, they realize effective instruction is not an accident or gift of birth. It must be developed and worked on, and if even good teachers must continue that effort, the less effective ones had better get busy themselves. The involvement of good teachers from the beginning tends to make interactions about instruction more constructive. Good teachers emphasize the positive, and to some extent that dampens the heavy cynicism often expressed by ineffective, disillusioned instructors. If faculty members with varying degrees of effectiveness are involved in activities, all worry much less about what others will conclude about their participation. Finally, when the good teachers are enthusiastic and pronounce the activities worthwhile, the less confident instructors are thereby encouraged to become involved. Moreover, instructional quality at an institution will increase most dramatically if all the teachers improve, not just the ones who need it.

In sum, then, instructional improvement needs to be mandated independently of need. To improve, according to one Webster's definition, means to "enhance in value or quality." That definition implies already present value and quality. Those encouraging improved instruction need not tackle the question of how much value and quality. Improvement can be justifiably advocated as something for all.

Putting the Faculty Member in Charge of the Improvement Process

A second strategy, putting the individual teacher in charge of his or her own improvement, also has interesting ramifications in terms of the role it forces instructional improvers to assume. Even though these individuals are the ones advocating better teaching, in many instances having received instructional improvement (from an institutional perspective) as an assigned responsibility, they must relinquish control of the improvement process and instead put faculty members in charge of their own efforts to teach more effectively. What this means, why it needs to be done, and how it encourages participation and overcomes resistance bears further elaboration.

Quite simply, putting faculty members in charge of instructional improvement means that they make decisions as to the *extent* of their involvement. If during a given semester, a faculty member decides time permits only the reading of short articles on participation strategies, that decision stands. When faculty members are in charge of the improvement agenda, they make the decisions about *what* needs to be improved. The improvement process proposed in Chapter Three helps to inform those decisions, but the faculty members involved identify the problems. Finally, the instructors involved identify the *means* by which the improvement will occur. If they think that they can solve the difficulty they have in holding student attention by viewing videotaped teaching samples or having students complete open-ended questionnaires or doing something else, those encouraging the improvement work with the faculty members to locate and use the selected method.

Another important aspect of putting faculty members in charge of the improvement process involves recognition of their possible need for confidentiality. For example, as further elaborated in Chapter Four, diagnostic, descriptive student evaluation data that a faculty member is collecting for the purpose of enlarging his or her understanding of the impact of certain instructional practices should never find their way into a promotion and tenure dossier, unless the faculty member puts them there. Such data should not be shared with others unless the faculty member does the sharing.

Why is this approach recommended? Because it recognizes a basic truth about improving teaching. Faculty must be in charge of the process because better teaching cannot be done by one party to another. Those interested in improving instruction may make all sorts of recommendations or see precisely how a given faculty member's teaching could be bettered, but only one person in the world can make the necessary changes and that is that faculty member. Improving teaching is very much like teaching students. We do our best to make the content understandable, to make students see its value and importance, to create a climate in which students can experience the content safely. When all is said and done, however, it is the student and the student alone who does the learning. Similarly, it is the teacher alone who changes the teaching.

There are several reasons why putting the faculty member in charge of the improvement process decreases resistance and motivates faculty participation. First, to the extent that a faculty member is in control of a situation, the degree of threat diminishes considerably. Faculty members now control *how* they find out about their teaching, to some degree *what* they find out, and finally *what they will do* about what they have learned. If they need to protect themselves, especially at the beginning, this approach permits that. Being in the driver's seat adds considerably to faculty confidence and motivation.

The approach also increases motivation because faculty members who make the choices for themselves will select improvement methods of perceived value to them. This increases the likelihood that the college teachers will complete the improvement activities. Faculty members will choose to do what they are interested in doing. In the end it boils down to the difference between doing what one has to and doing what one wants to do.

Moreover, what faculty find out about their teaching via methods of their own choosing, they will look at much more seriously. If they ask recent graduates about the merit of their course, they ask because they value and therefore will attend to the opinions of those former students. Both this advantage and the preceding one relate to the difference between intrinsic and extrinsic motivation and the motivation that energizes faculty in ways that eventually improve their instruction.

But what about objectivity? Can instructors see their teaching for what it is? Although a definitive yes is impossible, college teachers' objectivity is cultivated by this approach in three different ways. First, they control how much of their teaching they confront. A total confrontation is not required as a prerequisite first step. Often faculty are afraid to take more than a quick look at their teaching for fear of discovering some great heretofore unknown incompetence. In the majority of cases, however, the quick look is not going to reveal some stark and telling inadequacy. When looking, say, at how they use questioning strategies, faculty are more likely to discover bits and pieces, techniques that work sometimes and not others. Viewing teaching at close range and in parts is not likely to be threatening, and as a result faculty are encouraged to look still further. Moreover, the view from inside is obviously incomplete. Questioning techniques in and of themselves, for example, do not make much sense unless they are seen in the context of the structure of the material for a given day. In other words, in order to understand the whys and wherefores of a particular set of questioning strategies, faculty must look further at their teaching.

Second, objectivity is cultivated by the confidentiality associated with the process. Because the look at the teaching is not for the benefit of anyone other than the particular teacher, that privacy encourages realistic assessment. There is no need to lie to the self for the sake of others. Finally, the particular process proposed in Chapter Three further cultivates objectivity by creating a detailed sense of instructional awareness and then balancing self-perceptions against information acquired from others.

Offering Support to Any and All Faculty Efforts

At this point, the role of the instructional improver in the improvement process gets defined and gains considerable substance. For all sorts of reasons, faculty cannot be set on the quest for better teaching unaided. To begin with, as already noted in Chapter One, faculty are not trained to teach and teach relatively unaware of how they do it. They teach oblivious to research on teaching and learning and in many cases do not know that valuable instructional resources exist or where to find them.

Can faculty members legitimately be put in charge of the improvement process with such questionable qualifications? The answer is yes. They can be put in charge of the process, but only if the institution provides resources and services that support improvement efforts. Most commonly the task of providing the necessary resources and services falls to the instructional improver. Several different dimensions of the improver's role are important when the improvement responsibility belongs to the faculty member and the improver offers support to the effort. Instructional improvers must be knowledgeable about resources and able to direct faculty members to relevant information. They must act as guides, showing faculty the different routes to the objective and identifying the dangers and directness of each. They must also be advisers, making recommendations. Certainly the faculty member whose students do not participate should be advised that effort devoted to making a new overhead transparency is not likely to cure participation problems; more effective alternatives must be identified. Finally, those concerned with instructional improvement must provide encouragement and inspiration when faculty members discover the road is long and not without pitfalls.

In essence, then, the instructional improver acts as a consultant, not an implementer. In support of faculty efforts, the consultant offers expert advice and an honest assessment of what needs to be done and has ideas as to how the job can be accomplished. Literature on consultancy can be helpful to those wishing to learn more about the details of this role (Bergquist, 1979; Boud and McDonald, 1981; Carrier, Dalgaard, and Simpson, 1983). Addressing the specifics of consultative techniques for faculty and instructional developers, Lewis and Povlacs (1988) have assembled a collection of practical and theoretical readings that elaborate still further on the consultancy aspects of instructional improvement.

But is it enough simply to support faculty improvement efforts? Will faculty members decide to avail themselves of the resources offered and the advice given? Yes, for a number of reasons. Faculty members do not want to teach badly, even the ones who do. Bad teaching has too many negative consequences for the person doing it. Bakker and Lacey (1980, p. 36) reach the same conclusion: "Faculty generally want to do well at their teaching out of integrity more than from desire to keep a job. To be teaching poorly and not to know what to do about it is a kind of hell." So in spite of assumptions, characteristics, and less than supportive environments, most faculty members are not interested in teaching badly.

Moreover, faculty are more likely to take advantage of support if the instructional improver takes a proactive stance. Supporting faculty efforts does not mean sitting back and waiting for college teachers to make their needs known. What the instructional improver can do for faculty is advertised. He or she may suggest two or three good techniques for encouraging student participation. If the techniques are not terribly time consuming, most faculty will be willing to give them a try. Most would like to do a better job of encouraging student involvement. Many faculty members teach without a great deal of effectiveness because they really do not know how to teach otherwise. If the support is there and the choice to use it is theirs, most faculty members will avail themselves of the opportunity.

Instructional improvers can better understand their role if they think about faculty as students and approach getting college teachers involved much as they would approach encouraging students to learn. Instructional development is at heart a teaching task. In addition, faculty are the kinds of students we all love to teach. They are by nature independent learners, inquisitive and curious, and often highly motivated and self-directed once they get turned on to a topic. The literature on adult education can prove a valuable resource to people designing programs and activities aimed at helping faculty improve their teaching (see Knowles, 1980, or Zemke and Zemke, 1988, for example). When faculty members are shown the challenges and rigor of teaching, the intriguing nature of the phenomenon, and the importance of their role, they often get intellectually hooked and will devote themselves to understanding how good teaching works.

One can, of course, study teaching in the abstract, but because faculty members teach regularly, they have easy access to an arena in which they have the opportunity to translate theories into practices and analyze their effects. Other chapters of this book propose a variety of ways and means this intellectual interest can be stimulated, but for the moment the point is to show how and why faculty will avail themselves of resources on teaching. At a very fundamental level, most want to teach with at least some degree of effectiveness and most are eager learners.

Making instructional support available to faculty members can be motivational as well. At most institutions faculty have taught without support and in climates where instructional excellence is expected but not generally cultivated. Having someone knowledgeable about teaching available, seeing that the institution is willing to devote some resources (even modest ones) to support improvement efforts, and recognizing that to teach well college teachers do need support, all encourage faculty participation. So long as the support is offered freely and is not forced upon anyone, it also helps to overcome faculty resistance. There ends up being nothing to resist.

Believing That Faculty Members
Can Improve Their Teaching

Because faculty members are not trained to teach and often teach without a lot of instructional insight, many do not feel confident about their ability to change the way they teach. In the absence of that confidence, the conviction of the instructional improver can be especially persuasive to the faculty member contemplating making the effort.

Does a belief in the ability of faculty members to improve rest on a firm foundation? Can they in fact change in ways that increase their effectiveness? Yes, they can. Look again at the ingredients or components of effective instruction. They can be presented to faculty as acquirable skills. For example, most lectures can be presented so that their structure or organization is clearer to students. Lecture previews can be included, main points prepared on an overhead transparency, and more obvious transitions added. Students can be questioned for feedback as to their understanding of the structure. These are easy additions to the teaching style of most instructors. Although not all aspects of instruction can be improved as easily, merely altering mechanical aspects such as these will improve the instruction to some degree.

Believing in faculty members (just as believing in students) empowers them. They are motivated not only to participate but to succeed. This leads to another approach, more difficult for the instructional improver to be convinced of, but equally effective in motivating participation and overcoming resistance: a belief that faculty members want to improve. One can summon much evidence to the contrary, but the case is not closed. Faculty would not be in education if they did not have some fundamental commitment to the enterprise. As already noted, they do not want to teach badly, which admittedly is still recognizably different from having a commitment to instructional improvement. But perhaps it is possible for instructional improvers to know in their hearts the reality yet still in their interactions with faculty members to assume that they want to improve. The number of instructors who respond favorably to that approach may indeed be the evidence needed to ground this belief in fact.

Summary

The purpose of this chapter is to begin to show how the barriers and impediments to instructional improvement can be overcome. That process starts by encouraging faculty participation in the effort and overcoming initial resistance. The chapter proposes and elaborates an important but difficult role for would-be instructional improvers. Most fundamentally it challenges them to motivate faculty members instrinsically and suggests four approaches to help accomplish that objective. How instructional improvers might use these approaches is further explained in the context of an improvement process proposed in the next chapter.

3

◆◆◆◆◆◆◆◆◆◆◆◆◆◆◆◆◆◆◆◆◆◆◆◆◆◆◆◆

Improving Teaching:
A Five-Step Process

ARMED WITH a clear understanding of what stands in the way
of better college teaching and having considered strategies whereby resistance and participation can be impacted, we next need to
consider the actual process of improving instruction. Specifically,
how do faculty members go about improving their instruction?
What do those advocating better teaching suggest they do?

Unfortunately, some current approaches taken by faculty
and those working with them are troublesome. For example,
there is a tendency to focus on improvement activities in a sin-
gular, isolated sense. The literature on instructional development abounds with good ideas, each tending to be a specific
remedy, many being single-shot, quick fixes as opposed to more
general approaches that prescribe sustained efforts. The problem
is not with the activities themselves but rather with what they
and the people who use them presume about teaching and how
to increase its effectiveness.

Not one or even two activities are "right" or "best" for all
instructors, for all institutions, or for all instructional situations.
The improvement of instruction is just not this simple. However,
when faculty members, department heads, or interested administrators happen across an idea they find appealing, they often
tend to be converted and to start proselytizing. The way to better teaching lies in review of videotaped teaching samples, or
diagnostic student evaluation with consultation, or seminars on
course design, or mentoring with master teachers, or whatever
the favored strategy happens to be. *All* of these are possible ways
to better teaching, made "right" or "best" only after they have

been carefully matched with the instructional needs of the teacher, course content, and instructional setting.

Moreover, those who advocate independent activities are easily entrapped by the fantasy that teaching ills can be fixed quickly and easily — all you need to do is X and the problem is gone, forever. Sometimes a particular activity does make a big difference, especially if the problem tends to involve some mechanical aspect of teaching, such as annoying mannerisms or repetitious phrases. Excellence in the more significant aspects of teaching, such as creating a climate for learning or encouraging student involvement, is not easily achieved through passing participation in an instructional improvement "activity." When an activity becomes the single solution to all instructional ills, it reinforces an inaccurate and oversimplified conception of the teaching phenomenon.

In addition, college teachers often take a kind of hit-or-miss approach to instructional improvement rather than a considered and systematic one. Once again, student evaluation results frequently encourage this kind of haphazard approach. The results identify a problem abstractly, for example, an instructor attitude toward teaching the course, but do not name the specific instructional behaviors, policies, or practices that are causing students to conclude the instructor has a bad attitude. So instructors hazard a guess or two as to what might be causing the problem and try to do better next semester. They may take the same approach in response to a critical comment from a colleague or an isolated student. Unfortunately, instructional improvement is not a game like pin the tail on the donkey. There are more effective ways of attaching solutions to problems.

Faculty should systematically approach the process of implementing changes in how they teach. They need to view the process as an ongoing one. Teaching never gets "fixed" in any permanent, lasting way. They also need to make choices not on the basis of the appeal of a particular approach but because it fits the way they teach, what they teach, and the setting in which they teach.

Despite these needs, few instructional improvement processes have been proposed; none has yet been subjected to research analysis. However, given what is known about faculty motivational problems, college teachers' current approaches to instructional change, and behavior change generally, let us propose a five-step process as one means faculty might use to guide their pursuit of better teaching.

Steps in the Process

First, faculty members develop instructional awareness, a clear understanding of the instructional strategies, techniques, and practices they use and the assumptions about teaching and learning implicit in them. *Second,* they gather information from students and peers to accomplish three objectives. The input from others (a) clarifies and elaborates further the instructor's own understanding of his or her teaching; (b) it offers feedback as to the impact of the policy, practice, behavior, or activity on the person offering the input; and (c) it generates a pool of alternative ideas — other (and perhaps more effective) ways to accomplish the instructor's objectives. *Third,* faculty members make choices about changes. This involves identifying the teaching strategies, techniques, or practices to be changed and the instructional alternatives that are appropriate solutions for the particular teacher to try. *Fourth,* the faculty member implements the changes systematically and incrementally. *Fifth,* the faculty member assesses the impact of the alterations. The goals and activities appropriate for each step are summarized in Table 1, and the activities are elaborated on in subsequent chapters. Let's now look at each step in more detail.

Step One: Developing Instructional Awareness. The objective in step one is to have faculty members encounter themselves as teachers. Despite their extended and personal involvement with their own instructional activities both inside and outside class, most college teachers remain unaware of how they teach. At the first level, their lack of awareness is literal. They teach not knowing what nuts and bolts hold their teaching style together. Many have never given thought to when and where they move, how many questions they ask, or where and when they use examples.

Table 1. Steps in an Instructional Improvement Process.

Step 1 Develop Instructional Awareness	Step 2 Gather Information	Step 3 Change, Make Choices	Step 4 Implement Alterations	Step 5 Assess Effectiveness
Goal: to enlarge, clarify, and correct my understanding of how I teach	Goal: to compare my understanding of how I teach with the feedback of others	Goal: to decide what to change and how to change it	Goal: to incorporate changes in my teaching	Goal: to determine the impact of the alterations
Activities	Activities	Activities	Activities	Activities
• Use checklists to guide self-observation and personal reflection • Review videotaped samples of my teaching • Read to stimulate thought and reflection • Review course materials	• Use forms to gather formative feedback from students • Visit colleagues' classes and ask colleagues to visit mine • Talk with colleagues • Attend workshops and seminars to learn more about teaching • Interview past and present students about learning experiences in my course	• Identify *what* to change • Review possible policies, practices, and behaviors to be changed in light of educational objectives and priorities • Consider the order in which to change the instruction • Determine *how* to change policies, practices, and behaviors in light of information acquired in steps 1 and 2	• Incorporate changes systematically and wholeheartedly • Incorporate changes gradually	• Assess myself • Gather information from students and colleagues • If necessary, make change choices • If necessary, implement still further alterations • Assess any second-generation alterations

The lack of awareness exists at other and more significant levels as well. Many faculty do not know *why* they have assembled the collection of instructional policies, practices, procedures, and activities they regularly use. They do not see those instructional details in the context of what they believe about students and want them to learn from the course. Nor do college teachers see the details in light of the particular content configurations of their discipline or the course they are teaching. They may teach unaware that their beliefs are at odds with their practices.

Faculty need to begin the process of instructional improvement by enlarging, clarifying, possibly even rectifying their understanding of how they teach. Premise: They cannot possibly make reasoned choices as to what they could and should do if they do not have a clear understanding of how and why they teach as they do.

How can faculty be encouraged to cultivate this awareness? In all sorts of ways, which those advocating instructional improvement propose or even recommend but which faculty members select. Identifying instructional nuts and bolts and understanding how they hold the teaching together may be the place to start. Checklists such as the one in Appendix 1 or those proposed by Helling (1988) can be very helpful. Faculty can be counseled to review the questions just prior to teaching and then during class to begin to "check out" or "become aware of" how they handle the very mechanical aspects of teaching. Behaviorally oriented evaluation instruments such as the one developed by Murray (1985) and used in research to associate teaching effectiveness and instructional behaviors also help faculty cultivate this sense of instructional detail. If they find it too difficult to "look" at their teaching while teaching, private review of a videotaped teaching sample can be especially effective in revealing the details of their teaching style.

Awareness of the other levels is harder to come by, but it can be encouraged by provocative articles and by dialogue with colleagues and even with students. Fuhrmann and Grasha (1983, pp. 215–217) have developed a self-evaluation instrument that may be helpful. Those working with faculty at this step can be instrumental and proactive in raising the issues, asking the questions, and showing college teachers the ramifications of their classroom policies and practices in relation to instructional theory and research.

One especially important key to faculty success in this area involves making sure to whatever degree possible that these self-discoveries are free of judgments. If faculty at this stage get stuck trying to figure out whether what they do or believe is right or wrong, good or bad, they are headed down the wrong track. An excessively judgmental orientation inhibits openness and the ability to change.

Step Two: Gathering Information. Because teaching requires a great deal of self-investment, objectivity does not come easily. Thus, what faculty decide in step one about how and why they teach needs to be compared with the ideas, insights, and opinions of others. This information from colleagues and students needs to be gathered in three different areas: how the observer sees the instructor teaching; how a particular policy, practice, behavior, or combination of all three affects the observer; and what alternative (possibly more effective) policies, practices, and behaviors the observer thinks this instructor could (possibly should) be doing.

The college teacher needs to have others (colleagues and students) describe what they see happening in his or her classroom. This will help to clarify the faculty member's perception and will also serve to illustrate how the same set of instructional behaviors can be "seen" quite differently. In other words, it is not just the faculty member involved in improvement activities who may have trouble with objectivity. Colleagues "see" teaching through their own perceptions of what it could and should be, and students "see" what happens in a given class through a collection of experiences acquired in many other classrooms. For this reason, those who work to help faculty improve must recommend gathering information from different observers on different occasions.

Those observing the instruction should also describe how that instruction affected them. When observers experience instruction, they know for a fact how it affected them. When they suggest how the instruction affected others, they are drawing inferences, no longer stating facts. Moreover, teaching policies, practices, and behaviors have variable effects. They do not strike all who experience them in the same way. This means that most aspects of teaching are not right or wrong, good or bad, effective or ineffective in any absolute way. A less judgmental perspective more fairly represents the variable effects of instructional practices.

Finally, those offering input need to be asked to identify alternatives, other ways of accomplishing the faculty member's objectives. Unfortunately, this step is often omitted, leaving faculty members knowing how they teach and how that teaching affects others but with little or no sense of other possibilities.

Step Three: Making Choices About Changes. The next step in this improvement process prescribes making two choices about changes: *what* should be changed, and *how* it should be changed. What probably needs to be changed first are those instructional policies and practices that are at odds with what an instructor believes about students and learning (for example, aspiring to develop critical thinking abilities, but evaluating students with multiple-choice items that test recall) or those aspects of teaching at odds with the course content or instructional setting (for example, lecturing to ten students in a graduate seminar).

What about those aspects of instruction that do not affect the majority of observers favorably? They may need to be changed but not automatically, especially if they are the means an instructor uses to accomplish a top educational priority. For example, many students today do not respond favorably to essay exams. Nonetheless, that evaluation strategy does teach students to think more effectively than do many other evaluation techniques. Given a college teacher's instructional objectives and priorities, such exams may not be something that he or she can legitimately change. However, instructors should be advised to seek ways of changing surrounding activities — for example, giving students practice essay questions or providing examples of good essay answers — as a way of modifying the negative effects of a policy or practice that in all honesty cannot be changed.

On the other hand, not all that instructors do in the classroom reflect their priorities. If a practice provokes less than favorable responses and does not represent an instructional "bottom line," that practice may be the choice for change.

The choice of what to change need not always come from the negative perspective. The choice may be to change by doing more of some aspect of teaching that *does* sit well with an instructor's philosophy or with those who experience its effects. Instruction can be improved in two ways: by deleting those parts of it that do not work well and by expanding those aspects that are effective.

After having determined what to change, the next decision is how to change. Should the aspect of instruction be eliminated entirely? Eliminated but replaced with something else? Retained but reduced in emphasis? Retained but altered? And so on. Truly, the options abound, and faculty should be counseled that single right answers to instructional change choices are few and far between. Rather, all the options should be viewed as possibilities worth considering.

All options merit consideration in light of the instructional self that is discovered in steps one and two. For example, consider how that self-knowledge might be used to guide a change in certain presentational aspects of lecturing—for example, by adding some variety to enliven them. Maybe the faculty member should move about more. Maybe she should incorporate some gestures. Maybe she needs to vary her voice. All sorts of possibilities exist, and no one or two of the techniques guarantee success. Some are right for some teachers and wrong for others. If an instructor is most comfortable with his hands in his pockets, gestures are probably not the technique best suited to enlivening his teaching performance. What makes an alternative instructional strategy appropriate (worth trying) is its potential to fit into the natural style of the instructor.

An effective teaching style is always a genuine, authentic representation of the person involved. It is not some esoteric art form, some eclectic collection of affectations used in the classroom but nowhere else. Even after recognizing the public nature of the classroom and the inherent ethical constraints of the educational endeavor, faculty should still, to some extent, do what comes naturally when they teach. Using these guidelines, they should first try style alternatives that appeal to them, alternatives for which they feel an almost automatic affirmation: "Yes, I could do that."

Decisions about how to change aspects of teaching other than style should be made in the same way. For example, the content in various disciplines is configured differently and those inherent structures as well as course designs do affect how instructional strategies should be used. Certainly one change many college faculty could make would be to increase the amount of student participation in class. However, as one chemistry professor observed, "The periodic table is really not up for discussion." This does not rule out the possibility of student participation in chemistry courses, but it does say something about the kind of interaction a teacher can cultivate.

Step Four: Implementing the Alterations. In step four of the process, the changes get implemented, incorporated into the instructional practices of the faculty member involved. This works best when the implementation is systematic and incremental. The idea behind the systematic implementation of a change is simple. The change deserves to be given a fair chance. It should not be done halfheartedly or without careful preparation. What is being done differently ought to be the object of fixed and focused attention.

Implementation will also work best if it is incremental, if changes occur gradually, not all at once. Changing habitual responses and old, familiar ways of teaching requires concentration. If much has been changed, much concentration is required, and the level is difficult to maintain day after day in class. Implementing changes incrementally also contributes to faculty confidence. College teachers are coping with alterations of manageable proportions. The situation is under control. This increases the likelihood that they will continue the process of change.

When a faculty member is being counseled to change gradually, how does he or she decide what to change first? Most faculty gravitate toward what they perceive as the most serious problem, but that may not always be the best place to start. Success at the beginning of improvement efforts has large implications for subsequent involvement and commitment. If college teachers opt to make changes in an area where the chances of success are high (redoing, sprucing up, and otherwise spending time on overhead transparencies or some other fairly mechanical teaching activity), they become more committed to the process and feel more confident about their ability to handle the tougher problems.

Faculty members and those who work with them need to view instructional improvement, particularly the implementation step, as an ongoing endeavor, something that one never quite finishes. Instructors should adopt a tinkerer mentality toward their teaching. Much of what they do in the classroom works fine and has (in some cases) for many years. But like the faithful refrigerator or favorite jalopy, it must be looked after routinely. Most of the time the changes are small—minor adjustments or replacements. On occasion, something major goes awry. But the constant tinkering and preventive maintenance make the unexpected surprises fewer. The same things can be said of teaching and its improvement. Effective instruction results from continuing care, concern, and commitment.

The best part of the analogy is the joy the tinkerer derives from the efforts to keep something running smoothly. Teaching is a fascinating phenomenon when one contemplates how all its parts work together. Like refrigerators and jalopies, it can be repaired and thrives on attention. There is a sense of challenge, too. Sometimes the problem is clear, but the solution not as obvious. On the basis of previous experience and knowledge, the tinkerer makes some guesses about what might work and then tries them. Sometimes an unexpected or very simple adjustment makes all the difference. And when everything is working well, the tinkerer justifiably takes pride in having contributed to that efficient operation. Such an approach empowers teachers and makes their commitment to and involvement in the improvement process grow.

Step Five: Assessing the Alterations. Step five is in fact a combination of the preceding four steps. With knowledge of how and why one teaches derived from self-observation and information from others, the faculty member has made choices about changes and implemented them. At this juncture, the instructor must assess the effects of those changes. The first four steps of the process provide a method for doing that. The cyclical nature of the process bespeaks its continuity — the need for ongoing faculty involvement in improvement efforts. The justification is not remedial. Teaching does not deserve prolonged attention because it is profoundly bad. Rather, it deserves continuing consideration because, once fixed, there are no guarantees that it will stay that way and because, like many other activities, it can always be done better. Moreover, as faculty seek to do it better, students reap the benefits. That makes the effort worthwhile.

The Process in Action

But how does the instructional improvement process work? How does someone working with faculty members use the process to guide those interested in teaching better? Perhaps a case history (with identifying details altered) will illustrate the process in action. As with any illustration, this is one case in point; the process can be used in many different ways, depending on the role and style of the person working with the faculty member, the faculty member himself or herself, and the instructional needs, both as they are articulated by the faculty member and as they are perceived by the person working with him or her. Adherence to the steps as parts of an outline can be explicit or, as in the example, implicit, used to guide a faculty member's progress through a set of improvement activities. Recognizing the alternative ways in which the process can be used, consider this single description of how it works.

Della Carmichael chairs a twelve-member, math–computer science department at a medium-sized private liberal arts institution. She is meeting this morning with a second-year faculty member who has expressed some concerns about his teaching. Primarily, he is concerned that students seem so poorly prepared and motivated in his lower-division courses. Professor Fred Storitz arrives and the meeting begins.

Della opens the conversation by asking about Fred's classes this semester. He thinks they are going fairly well. She follows up by asking what text he is using in differential equations and how he uses the book in class. Fred names the text and says that he uses it primarily for homework problems. These he assigns regularly to students and then goes over the troublesome problems in class. Della asks Fred what he does when he goes over the problems in class. He looks as though he thinks the question is a bit strange. Obviously, he goes over problems by doing them on the board in front of the class. Della asks whether the students ask questions about the solutions. Fred says, "sometimes," but he knows that "rarely" is a more accurate answer.

At this point Della seems to change the subject and begins talking about an article she recently read on the value of having students doing at least some problem work in class. Fred agrees but points out what a time-consuming process that can be. Della responds that that is one of the reasons she liked the article. It suggested ways to incorporate in-class student work that might not be so time consuming. Fred asks more about the article, and Della quickly has the secretary make a copy for him.

Fred now raises the point of the meeting and expresses his concern. The students in his classes are not well prepared. They do not seem motivated and as a consequence are not doing well in the courses. This bothers him because these courses are prerequisites for all others in the department, and he wonders if his student evaluations might not be higher if he did not adhere to such high standards.

Della passes on the issue of evaluations and tackles student preparation and passivity. Her questions focus on Fred and what he does in class. Does he ask questions? When? Who answers? Do the students ask questions? Which ones? What kinds of questions? How is the homework handled? Why don't students get credit for it? Do homework problems appear on the exams? Fred wonders if this is some academic version of Twenty Questions, but Della stops long enough to explain that instructors need to know specifically what is happening in their classes and why they have chosen to pursue their educational objectives in that particular way. She talks about how easy it is for teaching behaviors to become routine and automatic, how often instructors teach as they were taught, and what poor justification that is for a set of instructional policies and practices.

But Fred counters that all he wants to know is how he can be more effective with his students. Della suggests there are all sorts of ways to increase effectiveness in the classroom, but to decide which ones are best or right for Fred, he must begin by clearly understanding his current instructional strategies and techniques. Fred has to agree that it doesn't make much sense to make changes if you don't know what you're changing from.

The questions continue. Della wonders how students study for the course. Do they work together? Do they do the homework regularly? Fred thinks some do, but he strongly suspects that the ones who need to do the homework most aren't doing it. Why? Della wonders. Fred doesn't know and launches into a diatribe about how students in college today seem to be there for all the wrong reasons. Della doesn't respond but inquires whether Fred has ever asked the students some open-ended questions describing how they study for the course. No, he hasn't. He's never seen a form for that. Della pulls a couple of forms from her file and suggests that Fred might consider using them, revising them if he thinks some of the questions don't apply or aren't relevant.

And does Fred know Stan Smiley? Not well. Stan did some interesting work with people from the learning center a few years ago. They helped him devise some assignments to use both in and out of class that Stan really thinks help weaker students. Fred might enjoy chatting with Stan, and Stan welcomes visitors in his class. It might be interesting for Fred to check out what Stan's doing. Della will mention to Stan that Fred may get in touch with him.

If it would help, Della tells Fred, she would certainly be glad to sit in on one of his classes and offer some reactions. But she also quickly notes that because she is department head, some faculty members are uncomfortable when she visits, so Fred should not feel compelled to ask her. Jill Stumpt, who teaches computer science, has helped a lot of new faculty, and

Della suggests that Fred might benefit from chatting with her and seeing how she conducts her classes.

The meeting ends. Fred leaves without the quick and easy answers he had hoped to get. There's got to be some trick to teaching students like his. Yet Fred does not feel upset or angry either. Della does have a way of making one feel that problems (even abstract ones in the classroom) can be solved, and what she has proposed does not seem all that bad. Fred decides to give it a try.

Three weeks later Fred schedules a second meeting with Della. He begins the conversation by tossing on her desk a folder of student answers to four open-ended questions he asked them. "Here, you make sense of these," he chides her. "They contradict each other, don't want any exams in the course, and think I ought to grade every single homework assignment." Della smiles and wonders if some of her students are taking Fred's courses. She volunteers to read through the comments and summarize what appear to her to be trends or especially good ideas. The two talk a little about the nature of this kind of data, how it can't be quantified and really isn't all that surprising that, given the differences among students, some activities work well for some and not so well for others.

Fred has had lunch with Stan, has visited one of his classes, and doesn't think their styles are at all similar. Della encourages Fred to explain why. It seems that Stan sort of wanders all around the room and calls on individual students, whereas Fred likes to stay near his notes so he can keep things in order. He's afraid he will intimidate students if he calls on them, and if he wanders all around the room, he loses track of where he is. In fact, so did Stan. He didn't solve the problems in the order that he said he would at the beginning of the class. Della asks if that confused the students. Fred doesn't think it was a major problem, and, boy, did the students in that class ever participate. Why? Della asks. Fred isn't sure but notes that the atmosphere was relaxed. What makes Fred say that? Well, he isn't sure. He could just look at the students and see they weren't afraid. Do students look like that in Fred's class? No, he doesn't think so. One simple thing he noticed: Stan smiled a lot — just a big friendly sort of smile every now and then. And you know, Fred admits a bit sheepishly, I don't think I do smile very often. Does he think he should or could? Della asks. Fred answers that he doesn't know but he's going to try in class tomorrow.

When Della asks Fred whether anyone has been in to see him teach yet, he shifts a bit nervously. He tells her he has been reviewing for an upcoming exam, it is just before break, and the present content is not typical of most of the course. A bit defensively, he suggests that everyone is so busy it seems like an imposition to ask. Della assures him that when he gets around to it, it will really be a valuable experience. A visit like this, she reminds him, has nothing to do with evaluation. The faculty is there as a friend and colleague, interested, concerned, and eager to help. Jill Stumpt doesn't even serve on promotion and tenure committees any more just so she can really help teachers in the classroom.

A week later Fred schedules another short meeting with Della to tell her that Jill visited his class and that he just can't believe all the ideas and insights he got from her. For example, Jill pointed out that when Fred asked for questions, he actually backed up and looked at his notes more than at the students. The next day in class he tried moving out from behind the table, smiling and looking directly at students when he asked a question. He couldn't believe that three or four people had their hands up.

Jill also thought Fred ought to start giving some credit for homework, even if he only randomly collects assignments. Della interrupts with the information that that comment is the one most frequently made by students on the open-ended questionnaire. Fred isn't convinced. All that grading adds to his already full work schedule, and besides that makes the homework busywork, just like in high school. Students have got to learn sometime that they don't get "credit" every time they do a little work. Has Fred ever told the students about his beliefs? Della asks. Well, no—it just doesn't seem like the kind of thing to take up class time with. Why not? How does Fred expect students to learn this lesson unless somebody explains it?

Fred wonders. But not for long. The next day in class as he finishes going over the homework problems, a student asks about getting credit for homework. Fred's first response is to answer briefly and move on, but he decides to tackle the issue. He moves around, sits on the corner of the table, and asks students to explain why they feel so strongly about the issue. Five hands are in the air immediately. One student talks about exam pressure and how hard it is when you only have two or three times in a class to show that you know the stuff. Homework is another way to show the instructor you are learning, at least trying. Another student honestly admits that the extra credit motivates. Still another talks about how homework takes time and students ought to get something for all that time. The vigor and intensity of the discussion surprise Fred. He goes further and asks the students how much the homework should count. Their proposals are more realistic than he expected, and one student even has a bright idea about having students grade the homework right in class as Fred goes over it. After class, he calls Della and asks whether she would mind meeting with him just once more.

Della begins the meeting by sharing with Fred a summary of the student responses to the open-ended questions. Somehow it makes a lot more sense to him seeing it all laid out on paper than it did shuffling through the individual comments. Fred thanks her, saying he will look over the material. Then he explains that what he really wants to discuss is what happened in class yesterday. He recounts the events and tells Della he thinks he ought to try handling the homework differently. What does she think he ought to do? Della replies that she doesn't know but suggests they go over some possibilities *after* Fred tells her what he wants homework activities to accomplish in the course. Well, he believes the activities should give the students practice in solving problems; they should develop students' confidence; they should prepare students for exams. Okay, now whatever Fred does with the homework, it needs to accomplish these objectives.

Della and Fred begin sharing ideas and considering possibilities. They discuss the merits of various approaches in terms of the objectives and the concerns Fred first expressed about his students. As the discussion continues Fred feels himself gravitating toward an approach in which part of the homework gets graded. He also likes the idea of assignments with some options, with students getting credit on the basis of the difficulty of the options they select. He recognizes that such an arrangement might challenge the better students while still helping less-prepared students. But Fred still can't decide how much credit to give. Della's advice is to try out something that seems reasonable and then see how well it works, both from his perspective and that of the students.

Della senses Fred's optimism and concludes the conversation supporting his decision but cautioning him not to expect this one change magically to erase all the preparation and motivation problems of his students. Fred agrees, but it feels good to be doing something more constructive than just complaining. He expects this to be the first change he makes, not the last one.

In conclusion, consider briefly how this instructional improvement process and case history illustration respond to the barriers described in Chapter One and the strategies for motivating faculty examined in Chapter Two. The process reflects the complexity of the teaching phenomenon and forces faculty members interested in improving to see it as an entity in its own right, not something subsumed within content knowledge. Notice how instruction, not content, was the focus of all exchanges between Della and Fred. By focusing attention on instructional details, this approach encourages faculty members to think of teaching in terms of policies, practices, procedures, activities, and behaviors. Notice how Della questioned Fred about what happened in his classes. The process addresses issues of faculty resistance and lack of motivation by putting the faculty members in charge. Notice how at every point of decision, Della deferred to Fred. She advised and counseled, but he decided. This process never raises the thorny evaluative issues that so frequently heighten faculty defensiveness and hostility. Rather, those who use the process (for example, Della) take the stance that instructional policies, practices, and behaviors have variable effects. If most of the time those effects are not favorable, instructors ought to consider changes. However, those changes must reflect an instructor's priorities and objectives. Notice how Della forced Fred to articulate his. Change must also fit comfortably and naturally into the teaching style and philosophy of the individual faculty member.

Summary

Because the five-step improvement process responds to identified barriers and incorporates the motivating strategies, it has the potential to improve instruction. The process is a simple one—but despite the complexity of the task it attempts to accomplish, its ability to adapt and adjust, accommodate and incorporate makes it a useful tool whereby better teaching can be accomplished.

PART TWO

◆◆◆◆◆◆◆◆◆◆◆◆◆◆◆◆◆◆◆◆◆◆◆◆◆◆◆◆◆◆

KEY ELEMENTS OF SUCCESSFUL INSTRUCTIONAL DEVELOPMENT

4

✦✦✦✦✦✦✦✦✦✦✦✦✦✦✦✦✦✦✦✦✦✦✦✦✦✦✦

Ongoing Assessment
and Feedback

THE INSTRUCTIONAL improvement process as proposed in Chapter Three uses the input acquired from others (students, colleagues, or both) to clarify, elaborate, and correct faculty members' understanding of how they teach. The nature of the data coming from others is therefore especially important. This inherent importance is magnified by the complexities associated with observing and assessing instruction and by the challenges of constructively conveying the information to the faculty member involved. Furthermore, the difficulties associated with these activities are generally compounded by the evaluative context in which they customarily occur.

This chapter aims to sort through this array of confounding variables with a single objective in mind: to show those working with faculty to improve their instruction how faculty members can acquire input so that it contributes constructively to the process. To begin, we explore the relationship between improving and evaluating instruction. How do activities associated with acquiring the sort of diagnostic and descriptive feedback needed to *improve instruction* and the presently common policies and practices used by institutions attempting to *evaluate instruction* affect each other? How does the "evaluation" being proposed here differ from what now occurs on many college and university campuses? After the relationship has been clarified, several guidelines can be proposed to ensure that faculty who seek this input will discover accurate and constructive ideas about how they teach. Finally, a variety of ways of acquiring input do exist, and this chapter concludes by describing a sampling of them, specifically those providing written input. Subsequent chapters describe other improvement activities designed to enlarge faculty understanding of college teaching.

The Nature of the Relationship Between the Evaluation and the Improvement of Instruction

Interest in the systematic evaluation of instruction has grown in recent years, although attempts to assess instructional effectiveness are by no means new. In the Middle Ages when faculty members, who dressed in full academic regalia, completed a lecture, they were expected to stand at the classroom door with mortarboard in hand. As the students left, they dropped coins into the mortarboard commensurate with their assessment of the lecture's worth. In other words, although college teachers and others may object to current evaluation practices, they were once worse.

The recent interest in evaluation grew out of the turbulent sixties, stimulated primarily by student pressure for greater involvement in the university's policies and activities that pertained to them. They wanted a voice, the opportunity to evaluate the instruction they experienced. This interest continues and is still growing. According to Seldin (1984), 67.5 percent of 616 four-year, undergraduate, liberal arts colleges surveyed in 1983 reported always using systematic student ratings in their evaluation of classroom teaching. That percentage had risen from 54.8 percent of those surveyed just five years earlier. Increased use of instructional evaluations has generated considerable research interest. Cashin (1988) reports that there are more than 1,300 articles and books dealing with research on student ratings of teaching.

Early advocates of student evaluation predicted that providing faculty members with student assessments would motivate them to improve and usher in a new era of college teaching. They were wrong, and understanding why begins to reveal something of the nature of the relationship between the evaluation and the improvement of instruction.

Most of the instructional evaluation that presently occurs is summative. It offers comprehensive assessments of instructional competence, the kind of data useful to those making personnel decisions. Typically, it compares: "Rate this faculty member in terms of others teaching at this institution." The data are most often acquired by means of bureaucratically efficient, machine-scorable short forms distributed to students at the end of the semester and processed and returned to the appropriate administrators and faculty after the course has been completed.

What the early advocates and many current proponents of summative evaluation assume is that giving this kind of feedback to faculty will enable them to improve. It will not, at least in any substantial way. Four reviews of research document only a modest impact: Rotem and Glasman (1979, p. 497) suggest "the existence of a minimal effect at best of feedback on instructional improvement at university level"; Cohen (1980, p. 321) reports that "On the average, feedback had a modest but significant effect on improving instruction"; Levinson-Rose and Menges (1981) are a bit more positive if the evaluative results are accompanied with consultation; and Menges and Brinko, (1986, p. 1) see consultation as a key variable in increasing the "positive but small effect" of ratings alone.

Despite the ineffectiveness of summative data to improve instruction substantially, it does make valuable contributions to the personnel evaluation process. Institutions must judge the performance of faculty members, and comprehensive assessments of instructional competence allow decisions in that area to be based on data, not gossip and hearsay. The problem is that comprehensive assessments do not give *faculty members* the information they need in order to make changes that will consistently increase their instructional effectiveness. An example will illustrate.

An instructor receives data indicating that on "attitude toward teaching this course," he ranks in the lowest ten percentile of all instructors at the institution. Such data clearly tell the instructor that some sort of attitude problem exists. But what attitude is offending the students? Moreover, attitudes are abstract, intangible things. They gain form and substance when they are translated into behaviors — actions instructors take in class. What is this instructor doing that students perceive as reflecting a bad attitude? Summative data offer no clues. And so the instructor who at this point is probably under pressure to improve has little recourse but to hazard some guesses and try to do better next term. As noted in Chapter Three, better ways of attaching solutions to problems do exist.

However, the matter is more serious than summative data not contributing much to improvement efforts. Some ways in which summative data are used actually cause harm by making faculty defensive, hostile, and much less favorably inclined toward improvement objectives. For example, some department heads list faculty members according to the last four digits of their social security numbers and rank them from top to bottom according to their "overall effectiveness" score. Others have been known to go even farther. They draw lines at points on the list and indicate that those above or below do or do not get merit pay raises. Both practices are empirically questionable, but more serious are the effects of such actions on faculty motivation and morale. Limerick (1987, p. 5) offers one assessment of the effects: "Over-accenting evaluations as a measure of success can create in teachers the same witless behavior that excessive concern with grades and grade-grubbing creates in students."

Thus for faculty at many colleges and universities, the relationship between evaluation and improvement has not been a constructive one. This fact should lead those interested in better teaching to consider other ways of managing the relationship. If instruction is to improve, teachers must have input as to the effect of their instructional policies, practices, and behaviors on students. But must that input always be collected in an evaluative context? Could it not be solicited and acquired in a context not of judging but of describing — first describing the aspect of instruction as it appeared to the observer and then describing the effect of that aspect on the observer who experienced it? Cashin (1988, p. 1) makes a similar distinction when he insists on using the term student *ratings* instead of student *evaluations*. "I suggest it is much more useful to think of these student reactions (and peer 'evaluation,' etc.) as data that need to be interpreted."

Is this a proposal for formative evaluation? Yes, to the extent that faculty need diagnostic, descriptive data on the impact of their instruction. No, to the extent that evaluation implies judgment, always focusing on whether the instruction is good or bad, right or wrong. In this regard, in the remainder of the chapter the word *formative* is used, but *evaluation* is not. More frequently, what is being proposed will be described as acquiring input or seeking feedback.

As for the relationship between evaluation and improvement, activities are needed within both arenas, but they must occur separately. Some institutions attempt to combine them. That approach is not wrong, but the effectiveness of activities in each of the areas is compromised when they are combined. The currently popular "cafeteria" style instruments are frequently used (not as they were designed) in ways that illustrate the compromises. (The original cafeteria system was developed in the early 1970s at Purdue; for a description of a more recent system, see Braskamp, Brandenburg, and Ory, 1984.) These instruments typically contain three different levels of questions. At the first level are the global, comparative questions (How does this instructor/course compare with all others at this institution?) that appear on all instruments. At the next level is a set of departmentally selected questions — items that reflect the nature of teaching excellence, content configurations, and instruction settings in the department. Such questions appear on all instruments administered within an individual department. Finally, from a pool of items, individual faculty members select a specified number of interest or value to them. It is at this third level that formative objectives are supposed to be accomplished. If the data are to be used in personnel decisions, submitted along with data from the rest of the instrument, however, faculty will feel strongly inclined to select items that will generate high marks, not items that may identify weaknesses or potential places for improvement. As a result, an instructor does not get the information about teaching that he or she really needs, and the institution gets a distorted view of the instructor's competence.

To be most effective, formative and summative activities must be separated (Abraham and Ost, 1978). That does not imply that the activities are unrelated. To make them totally independent of each other would inhibit their ability to make a difference in the overall effectiveness of instruction at an institution. To illustrate, if formative activities identify a number of areas where improvements can be implemented and a faculty member attempts to make those improvements, the changes must be reflected in the more comprehensive summative assessments. If the improvements do not make a difference in the evaluation used to make personnel decisions, the teacher will legitimately ask, "Why bother?" On the other hand, if summative assessments document a "need" to improve, but formative activities do not more specifically describe that need *and* propose alternative approaches, the question again will be "Why bother?"

From a theoretical perspective, the optimum relationship between efforts to evaluate instruction and efforts to improve it might be thought of this way: The summative assessment provides the overview, the global perspective on instructional effectiveness. Formative activities focus on the details, identifying and describing the effects of specific instructional policies, practices, and activities. The formative perspective provides a view of teaching from the inside — where the instructor sees how the parts interact to accomplish the larger teaching performance. But only looking from close up distorts the perspective and prevents the observer from seeing the larger context, so the observer must step back to see the big picture. In this way the summative and formative activities are separated but intrinsically a part of developing general and specific knowledge of the teaching self. To most effectively influence the instruction of an individual faculty member or an institution, both the summative and formative must be present.

The discussion of the current and proposed relationships between efforts to evaluate and efforts to improve has been lengthy, but understanding to at least some degree the difference between what is and what ought to be is essential if new improvement initiatives are to be more successful than previous ones.

Ways to Acquire Formative Feedback

Recall the purpose for which feedback is being sought: to help instructors clarify, elaborate, or correct their understanding of how they teach. Given that purpose and the background just discussed, what recommendations should those advocating formative activities make to faculty interested in improving the way they teach?

First, *let the instructor choose the ways and means.* Faculty paranoia, defensiveness, and resistance diminish to the extent that instructors control the feedback process. When they do, evaluation is no longer being done unto them. Letting faculty make the choices further illustrates how the improvement process comes under their aegis and control.

Some argue against relinquishing control to faculty members for fear that this will dilute the empirical requirements of a reliable and valid evaluation system. Research concerns about reliability and validity are beginning to filter through to practitioners, who now in general understand that evaluation instruments do not automatically produce good data. This being so, how can they legitimately place under faculty control the selection of instruments, the implementation of activities, and the interpretation of results? The answer McKeachie (1987, p. 4) offers involves further recognition of the distinctions between instructional improvement and instructional evaluation: "For personnel purposes, faculty and administrators rightfully have great concerns about the validity and reliability of evaluation data. These concerns are not as crucial when we are dealing with instructional improvement because the information collected serves simply as a source of hypotheses about what procedures an instructor might try in order to improve." That being the case, if the criteria used to measure the instruction are valid (that is, meaningful) for the individual instructor, that is of more concern than the instrument's absolute validity in terms of, say, research findings. Reliability of items on the instrument and between raters matters, but it matters far less when the data are not being used to compare individuals. If an instructor is advised to use the instrument in classes enrolling more than a few students and to use the instrument more than once or twice, a degree of reliability will be achieved. Thus if the instructor involved opts to create a new instrument designed to elicit input about the unique aspects of the course or instructional setting, in good conscience, he or she can be encouraged to use it. It is part of letting the instructor undertake the evaluation activities of his or her own choosing.

Obviously, encouraging faculty to make their own choices does not imply an anything-goes approach to gathering input about instruction. For example, formative instruments need to be designed, planned, tested, and revised. Formative instruments just like the summative ones do not automatically produce useful information about instruction. Wotruba and Wright (1975) describe aspects of instrument design that ought to concern instructors. Sommer (1981) illustrates the kind of care and attention necessary if feedback is to provide useful information across a teaching career.

Next, *encourage instructors to seek input from multiple sources.* As used here, *sources* has two different meanings. First, "multiple sources" indicates that the data (from students at this point) should be collected from more than one course. Instructors often teach very different courses, and to no small degree instructional strengths and weaknesses derive from the particular course in question. Even if an instructor teaches only one course or teaches the same course regularly, data should be collected from more than one section. What may be a strength in section one may be viewed as a weakness by students in section two or in the section taught the next semester. Teaching performances are in the main consistent, or stable, if the research jargon is preferred (Doyle, 1983; Marsh, 1984), but not always, and when the view of the teaching is formative, the perspective offers a close-up look at the parts. From that perspective, small differences do matter and will ultimately have an effect. The multiple sources, meaning more than a single student population, will help to ensure the reliability of the data.

The second use of "multiple sources" when applied to seeking input means using different types of instruments. These should encompass a variety of formats, as well as instruments with the same format but different questions, and instruments with the same format but a focus on different aspects of instruction. Some examples will illustrate. The two most common types of instruments are those with closed questions (to which students assign a number rating on the basis of how well they think the instructor does on that item) and those with open questions (to which students respond with written commentary, often on areas of their own choosing). Another, less common type of instrument is the inventory or checklist; here the evaluator indicates nothing more than the presence or absence of the behavior, practice, or whatever. Checklists focus on specifics and can be useful in developing a very descriptive sense of instructional awareness.

In addition to these different types, formative instruments can focus on particular parts or aspects of the larger teaching performance. For example, course material reviews can provide valuable insights about a course and an instructor. Short evaluation forms attached to exams can provide information as to students' feelings about the fairness, clearness, and comprehensiveness of an exam they have just taken. Instructors often have trouble finding textbooks that please students and still meet instructor expectations for course coverage. Perhaps this is because instructors so rarely involve students in textbook selection activities. How useful to be able to say to students beginning a course, "I have chosen the textbook for this course on the basis of reviews and recommendations I received from a student textbook review committee from the previous class."

Recommend formative activities that blend positive and negative feedback. This recommendation hearkens back to long-standing research on feedback (Barnlund, 1968, pp. 229–231) and the need for the recipient to obtain both positive and negative input. The objective is not a perfect balance but a blend of both. That goal makes a great deal of sense, especially when the objective is instructional improvement. Faculty are not particularly motivated to improve if they only find out what they are doing right. Too soon they become satisfied with their performance. On the other hand, if the feedback identifies only weaknesses, very soon they get discouraged and no longer seek the input.

The instruments and activities that faculty use should therefore provide both positive and negative input and not only for motivational reasons.

Teaching can be improved in two ways: Weaknesses can be eliminated, and strengths can be emphasized. Most often the emphasis is on the first way, and certainly that does work. Remove what is not effective and even if nothing else is added, the net performance will have improved. Moreover, weaknesses need to be eliminated. If they are not, even effective emphasis of strengths may not overcome their negative impact on total teaching performance. But the value of making strengths still stronger should not be overlooked. If something works in a classroom, perhaps it can be used more often or possibly a modified version can be developed for use at other times. Emphasizing strengths is particularly important when the overall teaching peformance is mediocre or poor. The motivation and ability of the weaker faculty member can only be enhanced by focusing, especially in the beginning, on strengths and working to employ them more effectively in the instruction. The poorer teacher then learns what success feels like and can probably tackle the weaknesses much more definitively.

Encourage faculty dialogue about the results. Research findings (Menges and Brinko, 1986) document a much more dramatic effect on subsequent evaluations if faculty members talk about the results. Consultation can be with a trained expert, someone from an instructional development program or center who will explore with faculty what the results mean. To date, however, there is no documented evidence that "expert" consultants are any more effective than faculty members themselves. In fact, faculty commitment to notions of collegiality may put peers in an even stronger position. Whoever ends up talking with the particular faculty member about the results needs to respect that person's confidentiality.

What needs to be discussed? The research that documents the positive effect of consultation on subsequent evaluations is not particularly helpful in answering that question. That is one of the areas Menges and Brinko (1986, p. 11), who reviewed thirty studies on the effectiveness of feedback, targeted for subsequent research. Faced with this paucity of evidence, they wonder if consultation is effective "merely" because it "insures that feedback is actively attended to and processed." That may be. It also may be that discussion helps because written input from students invites analysis. The data capture and freeze multiple reactions to a highly variable and dynamic phenomenon. What any given set of results "mean" and more importantly what an instructor should do about them does not generally jump out from the data. It is more a question of possibilities and of trying to figure out how to translate the results into specific behaviors. What is the instructor doing in class that results in this particular student response? Exploration of issues such as these is much easier when someone else can bounce back ideas and suggest alternative interpretations.

But the dialogue should not only be with colleagues and consultants; it should be with the students as well. Initially, instructors may not feel comfortable discussing the input with students, but they should be encouraged to aim in that direction even if at first all they do is thank students for taking the time to fill out the form. This discussion completes the feedback loop. Students see that instructors are interested, do take their input seriously, and will where appropriate try to make adjustments. That has got to be to an instructor's benefit when students complete the end-of-course or summative evaluations.

More important, instructors can solicit from students additional input — especially about bits of data that may be contradictory. If half the students like the homework and half object to it, an instructor can (and indeed should) confront the class with the contradiction. "What can we do to change this so that it works better for some but just as well for others?" Instructors can also ask students for clarifications as well as additional ideas for alternatives. Finally, instructors can use this dialogue to help students understand and more willingly accept some of the responsibility for the classroom environment. Truly, an instructor cannot do it alone. Students contribute in large and small ways to the overall learning atmosphere in a class. Responding to input from students about the class gives the instructor a perfect opportunity to offer students some feedback as well. The whole idea of this exchange with students is to get them and the faculty member to take seriously the need to solicit, provide, and respond to input about instruction.

Recommend that faculty acquire formative input during a course. It is more useful then. This is supported partly by research (Overall and Marsh, 1979), and partly by good old common sense. When an instructor collects student reactions during the course, he or she has an opportunity to make changes, to try alternative strategies. When the instructor receives the data after the fact, he or she faces a different class, which may be responding in different ways than the previous class. The impact and effectiveness of alterations are much easier to assess when the problem and solution are close at hand. Moreover, data collected during the course reinforces the ongoing nature of the improvement process. Instructors should routinely find out how a course is going during the semester. They can then respond to many of the objections students raise.

Be sure the formative feedback includes input about alternatives. One of the principal problems with evaluation (both summative and formative) activities today is that suggestions as to alternatives are not routinely included. The faculty member finds out what is and is not working but gains no information as to alternatives. For example, the homework assignments are not achieving the desired effects — students report that the homework assignments do not prepare them for the exam, the assignments do not make it easier to understand the material presented in class, and the students object to doing assignments that appear to count for nothing. Such input is valuable but incomplete because the instructor has no ideas, other than his or her own, as to what alternatives might increase the effectiveness of the homework in accomplishing course objectives. Certainly there is nothing wrong with the instructor's ideas, but faculty members do not always think of things from students' perspectives. Sometimes the students' ideas may be better than the instructor's. More important, instructors do not always have ideas as to alternatives. As already established, professors in general are not the most sophisticated or insightful of pedagogues. They really may not know what to do to make the homework more meaningful. In such a case, the importance of evaluators as sources of information about alternatives increases significantly. For this reason, instructors must be encouraged to request, indeed solicit, input about alternatives when they seek formative feedback.

Formative activities are not automatically effective in accomplishing their intended purposes. The ways in which they are used greatly enhance or inhibit their potential effectiveness. The intent of this section has been to identify some of the ways in which formative input can be acquired so that it contributes constructively and significantly to an instructor's efforts to teach more effectively. These general guidelines create an appropriate backdrop for the following discussion of specific types of instruments instructors can use to acquire formative feedback.

Kinds and Characteristics
of Formative Feedback Instruments

Four different types of formative feedback instruments are described in this section. Their characteristics, some advice about using them, and some examples are summarized in Table 2 and individually discussed below.

Closed-Question Instruments. Closed-question instruments use a predetermined and fixed set of items to solicit responses to certain instructor and course characteristics. Generally, responses are scored on a scale of one to three, one to five, one to seven, or some other combination. Samples of closed-question instruments abound. The following publications include sections that contain a variety of different forms: Bergquist and Phillips, 1975a; Centra, 1979; Roe and McDonald, 1983; Braskamp, Brandenburg, and Ory, 1984; and Miller, 1987.

When the objective is to improve instruction, there is no reason to "require" the use of a particular form. Rather, faculty members should be encouraged to review a variety of forms and to select ones that reflect their own instructional priorities and are suitable for the kinds of courses they teach. Instructors should also be encouraged to use or review (as models) empirically developed instruments. A great deal is known about constructing

Table 2. Formative Feedback Instruments.

Kind	Characteristics	Advice	Examples
Closed-Question Instruments (formative versions)	• Use a predetermined and fixed set of items • Individual items are scored on a scale • Results are easy to quantify • May be either formative, summative, or a blend of both • Tend to be longer and more specific, less judgmental, and more descriptive than summative instruments • Can offer input in many different areas on a single instrument	• Do not calculate institutional norms • Do calculate standard deviations • Encourage self-evaluation for comparative purposes • Do not discuss whether the results are good or bad	The following books include collections of samples (not all are formative): Bergquist and Phillips, 1975b; Centra, 1979; Roe and McDonald, 1983; Braskamp, Brandenburg and Ory, 1984; Miller, 1987
Open-Ended Instruments	• Contain items that encourage further response • Allow the focus of the answer to be determined by the respondent • The quality of the question helps to determine the quality of the answer • Generate a rich data pool • Are primarily valuable as a source of ideas • Produce a hodgepodge of results; are difficult to summarize and/or quantify	• Avoid extremely open-ended questions that encourage students to comment where they will • Use more narrowly focused questions • Encourage teachers to give students enough time to offer thoughtful feedback (not the last five minutes of a period) • Have instructors solicit the aid of a colleague in interpreting the results	McInnis, 1974; revised and expanded in Weimer, Kerns, and Parrett, 1988

Checklists and Inventories	• Look like closed-question instruments but do not contain rating scales • Establish the presence, absence, and extent of some concrete activity or behavior • Do not establish effect or impact of activity or behavior • Are good for developing instructional awareness	• Use when instructors are especially defensive • Use when instructors have inaccurate understandings of how they teach • Use in an observational context	"How Do You Teach?" (Appendix 1), from Murray, 1987; Helling, 1988
Focused Topic Instruments	• May contain closed or open questions • May be checklists or inventories • Focus on a particular aspect of instruction	• Help faculty members create their own • Do not use as first step in developing instructional awareness but as follow-up when the effect of some instructional policy or practice needs elaboration • Use to solicit input on the effectiveness of an alteration that has been implemented	• "Grade the Exam" in McMullen-Pastrick and Gleason, 1986 • Lecture techniques in University of London Teaching Methods Unit, 1976 • Discussion, lab, and studio experiences in Bergquist and Phillips, 1975b • Classroom environment in Fraser, Treagust, and Dennis, 1986 • Course materials review in Weimer, 1986

feedback instruments so that they reflect and appropriately weight the research-identified components of effective instruction. Although faculty members should be free to make choices (as opposed to meeting requirements), those working with them should make them aware that evaluation instruments are not all equal.

What if faculty members do not choose to use the "best" form in terms of providing input in areas where they most need it? So be it. If the form is one that a faculty member has selected and considers credible, she or he will look at the feedback much more seriously, and that is the essential first step in any improvement process.

The area in which college teachers and the instructional improvers who work with them may need help is in distinguishing between formative and summative instruments. Actually, few instruments are exclusively one or the other; rather, the matter is one of focus. In general, formative instruments tend to be longer, including specific items on a variety of different aspects of instruction. Formative items focus on details, on specific instructional policies and practices and their effects on students: "Students are encouraged to ask questions and are given meaningful answers." "Methods of evaluating student work are fair and appropriate." "Course materials are well prepared and carefully presented." Formative instruments include items that are more descriptive than judgmental. These examples illustrate the descriptive focus, which one can see when they are contrasted with more judgmentally focused items: "Course made interesting by instructor." This example also illustrates a more general than specific question. What it shows best, however, are a judgmental focus and why low scores tend to make instructors hostile and defensive. If the course was not "made interesting by the instructor," what is left to conclude about the instructor?

Faculty using closed-question instruments should be advised not to use comparative questions unless no other source of comparative data exists, and even then they should use such questions sparingly. Knowing how an instructor compares with other instructors can be fine, interesting, possibly motivational, but it is not useful when it comes to determining what needs to be changed and how. Moreover, comparative questions by their very nature arouse faculty defensiveness, which is not the attitude one wants to cultivate when instructional improvement is the aim. Nonetheless, some instructors gravitate toward such questions. If they insist on using comparative questions, even in their individual evaluation activities, the questions' potential to arouse emotional responses can be diminished by not calculating institutional norms. For example, students respond to the overall question "How does this instructor compare with others you have had?" or "Would you recommend this instructor to other students?" and the mean response is calculated for the instructor but not for the institution. That way, the issue of whether a 3.8 on a 5-point scale is above or below average, as high as it ought to be, is strictly a matter of personal interpretation. It should never be a subject of debate between those discussing the results.

This leads quite naturally to the discussion of norms and their role in the formative realm. Norms do provide useful comparative benchmarks, especially for faculty members who may be teaching with their heads in the sand. In general, however, numerical calculation should not be the focus of formative feedback. The point is not whether the 3.8 is a good score or whether it is better than the average score in the department. Those are summative concerns. In the formative realm the question is "What is the instructor doing or not doing that explains why the average is 3.8?" To instructors who want to talk about the scores, the questions are "Are you satisfied with the score?" "Is this an area you are interested in working on?" When those talking with faculty about results refuse to discuss whether the scores are good or bad, the faculty members themselves tend to back off and the discussion can then focus on how classroom activities, policies, and practices relate to the scores received.

Standard deviation data do serve formative objectives and should be considered by instructors looking at closed-question results. Simply put, standard deviations focus on the extent of agreement that exists between individual answers to the same questions. On a 5-point scale the mean may be a 2.5 with all the students selecting 2s or 3s; in that case, the policy or practice in question is having approximately the same effect on all the students. This cannot be said if some students select the highest rating, some the lowest, and others the ratings in between. The mean or average will still be 2.5, but students are not in agreement as to the effects of this particular practice.

What do standard deviation data tell faculty about implementing changes? The answer depends on the data, but here are some general guidelines. If the mean is 2.0 on a 5-point scale and most of the individual student ratings are 1, 2, or 3, that instructional policy or practice probably needs to be changed. In contrast, if the mean is 4.2 on the same scale and most of the individual student ratings are 4 or 5, that instructional policy or practice is positively affecting most students and should not be changed and perhaps it should be increased. If the mean is 3.0 but the individual student ratings vary widely, that instructional practice is having such mixed effects that the instructor would be best counseled to acquire additional input before implementing changes. If the instructor does incorporate changes, the individual student ratings may change but not the mean. In other words, those who responded to the instructional practice favorably now respond negatively and those who did not view it favorably before now do. The net effect is no change. It is probably impossible to satisfy all students, but one cannot even approach that ideal without discovering the details of the complaints and compliments.

Those who lobby in favor of calculating and distributing normative data do so because this sort of comparative information confronts faculty with reality and not all of them teach with a realization of how their instruction affects students. Such advocates may point out that on an instrument where data are not normed, faculty can look at an overall effectiveness average of 2.0 on the low side of a 5-point scale and figure that that is an above average rating. The point is well taken, but there are other ways of correcting faculty assessments that are not nearly as likely to engender negative emotional reactions and subsequent avoidance of further evaluation activities. For example, faculty using close-questioned, formative instruments can be encouraged to complete the same instrument they ask students to fill out. Faculty who hesitate to put themselves on the line can be advised not to answer on the basis of their own feelings but to try to guess what rating will be closest to the student mean. Many instructors find evaluation from that perspective almost fun and look eagerly to see how often they hit or missed. For new faculty members especially, the ability to "read" a class in terms of how the students are responding is a critical skill that they need to develop. Forcing themselves to predict student response on an instrument can be a valuable reality-checking experience that lets them know how well they can "read" student response.

When faculty fill out the instrument on the basis of how they feel about the class, the feedback is different but equally valuable. Perhaps they regard their experience in the class as positive, but students do not share that response. That does not deny the validity of a faculty member's experience. What it does is force the instructor to confront the question of how he or she can better communicate that positive experience to students. On the other hand, if the instructor tends to be negative and critical of what is transpiring in the class (perhaps because it is this person's first or fortieth time through a course) and his or her assessment falls well below that of the students, the teacher may be heartened to know that from the students' perspective things are not going all that badly. In all cases, the technique works well to provide a comparative benchmark that confronts the instructor with reality but does so without engendering defensive reactions.

One other alternative within the closed-question, formative instrument realm can be recommended: Encourage faculty to construct their own instruments. Most college teachers and those working with them shy away from this alternative, believing that the task is beyond them. Certainly instruments that will be used to generate data for personnel decisions need to be constructed and tested by measurement experts, but the empirical integrity of the instrument is not as important an issue in the formative realm. For the faculty member expressing a great deal of dissatisfaction with the instruments that have been used to assess his or her teaching, the possibility of controlling the content of an instrument can be highly motivational. Even for faculty who have been teaching for many years, the opportunity to ask what they have always wanted to know about their teaching may be too appealing to pass up.

When faculty members construct their own instrument, they can make it as sophisticated or elementary as they wish. The object here is to acquire input, not to evaluate the instruction. Faculty members should be encouraged to review a variety of instruments. They can then cut and paste individual items and sections together into a self-assembled instrument. There is one caveat with this approach: Frequently, the clarity of an instrument suffers when too many different question formats, types, and scales are included in it. Faculty should be advised to work toward a consistent format, rewriting questions they particularly like to fit the mold. One way to encourage such consistency is to provide faculty members with a pool of items, all worded similarly, and then let them assemble the items of their choosing on a blank instrument, possibly with a scale included or recommended. An example appears in Weimer, Kerns, and Parrett (1988b).

One faculty member who used this approach happened upon a unique iteration of the process when a student confronted him after class and asked why he did not have a question about X on the evaluation. The professor said that it had never crossed his mind to ask about X and wondered how many other questions he had never thought of. The next semester he selected ten items for the instrument and asked for student volunteers to whom he assigned the task of selecting ten additional items for inclusion. The professor noted that he learned almost as much about his teaching from the items the students selected as from the evaluation results themselves.

By now it should be obvious that closed-question instruments offer faculty members a great deal of important feedback about their instruction, but only if the instruments are used in ways consistent with formative objectives. The fundamental question to ask of all activities associated with closed-questions instruments is this: How is the data going to support, assist, and encourage the individual who seeks the input to better understand how he or she teaches? The data must contribute to the improvement process.

Open-Ended Instruments. Open-ended instruments contain items that encourage further response and allow the respondent to determine the focus of the answer. These are the instruments that encourage students (and sometimes colleagues) to comment where they will about the instruction's effects on them. The key to acquiring useful information from students who complete these instruments relates to the kind of questions they are asked. In other words, the quality of the question to a large degree determines the quality of the answer. The principal value of open-ended questions lies in their ability to generate a rich data pool — their potential as an idea source. The problem (serious from the summative perspective, but not the formative) is that the data elicited are not easily quantifiable. Both the key to successful questions and their principal value merit further discussion.

Open-ended questions are often appended to summative instruments and some with a formative focus as well. The use of such questions in summative instruments again illustrates how combining formative and summative objectives to some degree compromises both. Open-ended questions more naturally fall into the formative realm (Braskamp, Ory, and Pieper, 1981). The focus is on details. They produce a hodgepodge of results that are difficult to summarize and difficult to integrate into comparisons of different faculty members. These results do not expedite personnel decision making.

However, the use of open-ended questions in the formative domain is not without problems as well. The most serious difficulty often derives from the questions themselves. They are too open, in effect giving students license to comment wherever and however they will. Take, for example, the frequently paired query "What did you like most/least about the course?" The question invites students to comment on the instructor's dress or hair color, on the presence or absence of other types of students in the class, on the time or location of the class, and on a host of other, in the main, irrelevant and uncontrollable (at least from the instructor's position) variables. Moreover, students are encouraged to make these comments from behind a cloak of anonymity.

If part of the whole evaluation enterprise is to encourage students to take their assessment responsibilities seriously, asking them questions that make it very easy to provide less than constructive input and allowing them to offer that feedback without fear of reprisal, does not seem like the most effective way to teach that lesson. Moreover, the effects of such irresponsible commentary on faculty members should not be underestimated. Despite the fact that an instructor may laugh along with everybody else in response to a particularly bizarre comment, telling that instructor that the best way to improve the course is to "use the lecture notes for toilet paper" is neither funny nor constructive. Open-ended questions that allow, indeed encourage, this kind of response add still further to an instructor's inherent vulnerability. They may well be one of the reasons why evaluation activities in general are not well received by most faculty members.

For formative open-ended questions to be effective, they need to be narrowly focused. The reasons for collecting formative feedback bear reiteration. In terms of the improvement process proposed, this input provides the instructor with the diagnostic and descriptive data that helps him clarify and elaborate his understanding of how he teaches and contributes to his search for alternative strategies and approaches. Given that purpose, the questions of most value will be those that focus on instructional behaviors: what the instructor is doing and how he might do it differently. Questions such as the following (McInnis, 1974) illustrate the desired narrowed focus of appropriate open-ended questions. "When do you find the instructor to be most/least helpful in your learning?" "When do you feel the most/least intellectually stimulated by this course?" "When do you want most/least to discuss the material in this course?"

Analysis of the comments students write in response to open-ended questions confirms that they tend not to offer much input as to alternatives (Braskamp, Ory, and Pieper, 1981). That may be because the questions inquiring about improvements are poor questions. Some instructors have used the following approach and have been very impressed by the quality of the student response it generated. The instructor presents the students with four aspects of instruction, say, student participation, relevance of lecture content, usefulness of homework problems, and clarity of course objectives. The instructor tells the students that she is trying to increase her effectiveness in each of these four areas and would like to have suggestions of specific activities, strategies, or techniques the students believe she could use to accomplish that goal in this course.

It may also be that when students are asked to offer input about alternatives or to respond to focused, open-ended questions, they suffer from the same lack of instructional awareness that plagues instructors. Students, too, have not been trained to observe instructional processes or to describe them. Sometimes vague, imprecise, even insensitive descriptions result. One student reported to the author that he did not really like a certain professor. Why not? "Oh, I don't know, I just get bad vibes from him." The point to the student was that the professor was trying to make some changes in his teaching, and the student's suggestion was that the professor not vibrate badly in front of students. Students, just as faculty, can and should be encouraged to think and talk about teaching in more concrete ways. That they do not provide specific input in response to open-ended queries is not a problem with this method; it results from the way the method has been used to date.

Faculty members who are going to use this particular feedback mechanism need to understand that students cannot be expected to respond to such a questionnaire in the final two minutes of a class period. If they are to respond thoughtfully, they must be given enough time to think. Some instructors encourage students to take the questionnaires home; here the problem is getting them back. This may not be as much of an issue as many instructors think it is. The objective with open-ended instruments is quality, not quantity, of data. Three or four carefully completed forms may well be worth more than eight or nine with hastily scribbled one- or two-word responses.

Anyone looking at open-ended data must always keep in mind the principal value of the data: to be an idea resource. Faculty members tend to want to quantify all data, and answers to open-ended questions are no exception. College teachers are interested in counting up comments and end up anguishing over the one comment that seems to fit between two categories. Certainly the data should be examined for trends — the same observation being made more than once — but when people become obsessed with counting comments, they miss the more intrinsic value of the data. Sometimes only one student will make a given comment, but because the observation is phrased in a particularly insightful and telling way, it may open up a whole new vista of understanding for a faculty member. Good ideas for alternatives are not generally shared visions; they are much more likely to be the insight of one perceptive observer. Closed-question instruments are much better sources of information for the "degree-to-which" type of data. Open-ended questions should be the means to infuse teaching with fresh ideas.

Instructors can also increase the value of open-ended data by soliciting the aid of a colleague in interpreting them. Two heads are better than one, and the colleague may better understand what the student is trying to say. After all, the colleague does have a certain objectivity the instructor may lack. That objectivity can also be helpful to the instructor when it comes to putting individual comments in perspective. Sometimes students are basically disgruntled and unhappy. They may be impossible to please. A colleague can encourage a teacher to put individual comments in a larger context.

Open-ended questionnaires also claim the advantage of versatility. They can be administered much like the more formal, end-of-course evaluations are, or they can be used on the spur of the moment, depending on the particular situation. Suppose an instructor has put a new twist on homework problems or reading assignments and wants some feedback on the effectiveness of the new strategy. The instructor can solicit input from students by writing two or three open-ended questions on an overhead transparency and asking students to take five minutes to write down their reactions. Some instructors find this spontaneous, specific feedback so useful that they make "reaction sheets" or "suggestion/question" boxes a permanent feature of the class. Chemistry professors Strauss and Fulwiler (1987) write in detail of their experiences acquiring student feedback via a cardboard box they labeled "thoughts, questions, concerns, critiques, and commentary." They incorporated student responses right into the course by transferring the input in the students' handwriting onto overhead transparencies and then responding to the issues raised. The professors heartily endorse the activity, especially for large introductory courses.

Open-ended instruments offer faculty a wide variety of alternatives and a rich source of ideas and information. To best achieve formative objectives the questions need to be focused on particular aspects of the instruction. Faculty need counsel about looking at the results of open-ended questions. These are not data to quantify but rather results to "pan" for nuggets of insight and possibility.

Checklists and Inventories. Checklists and inventories look like closed-question instruments but for one difference. They do not (or should not) contain scales that require rating. Checklists and inventories establish three things: the presence, absence, and extent of some concrete activity or behavior. They are especially effective in developing instructional awareness, making instructors realize what they do or do not do in the classroom. But checklists and inventories do that without establishing the impact of the behavior. They only describe, never judge. From checklists or inventories, instructors can learn what they do, but they cannot discover whether their activities are effective. This makes these instruments a mixed blessing.

Nevertheless, checklists and inventories can make valuable contributions to the improvement enterprise if they are used with understanding. In two particular cases, nothing can beat them. The first is the case of the very defensive faculty member who probably has a long history of not doing well on evaluations. This is the rationale: "We think you ought to find out what you're doing in the classroom. We're not interested (and you shouldn't be) in whether it's good or bad. Long before that we need to find out *how* you teach." The faculty member may have all students, a selected group of them, a colleague, or an instructional developer complete the inventory or checklist. These devices identify aspects of teaching and behaviors associated with them. They describe the mechanics, and that is the best and safest place to begin with faculty who have been burned in previous evaluation activities.

Another case in which checklists and inventories make special contributions is with instructors who have inaccurate understandings of how they teach. Department heads sometimes encounter such faculty members during an annual appraisal review. For example, summative student evaluation results are not especially positive, but when confronted with the results, the instructor describes teaching techniques and strategies, behaviors, and policies that sound appropriate and potentially effective. How can this be? Who knows, but independent of any further summative results, a checklist or inventory can effectively document the presence of what the instructor claims.

Checklists and inventories work most effectively in an observational context, when the teaching in question is being observed. Videotaped teaching samples are especially amenable to review with checklists and inventories. The use of videotaping as an improvement activity is discussed in Chapter Five, but in this context it is easy to see how the sample can be reviewed by the instructor, a colleague, an instructional developer, or any combination of the three and the presence or absence of certain behaviors documented. The beauty of the method is that the results are not debatable. Either the instructor asked students questions or he did not.

Therein, too, lies the inherent weakness of checklists and inventories. They offer no help in assessing the impact of the behaviors used, although some researchers (for example, Murray, 1983) are currently working to develop checklists that contain behaviors associated with effective instruction. Even so, checklists cannot be used exclusively because the faculty member only finds out how he or she teaches. As necessary a first step as this is, if it is the only step, improvement objectives will probably not be accomplished.

One final factor limits the value and use of checklists and inventories. Not many exist. Of the few that have been published, consider the checklist "How Do You Teach?" (Murray, 1987: Hellig, 1988), which appears in Resource A. Researchers interested in assessing the instruction of primary and secondary school teachers have developed and use a variety of behavioral observation systems that can be helpful in the design and use of behavior inventories at the postsecondary level. Six of these systems are discussed in McNergney and Carrier (1981).

Focused Topic Instruments. Focused topic instruments may contain closed or open questions; they may be checklists or inventories. What makes them unique is their focus on a particular aspect of instruction. Their aim is to look specifically at one part of the total instructional performance, not to develop a comprehensive understanding of instructional effectiveness. Some examples will illustrate this type of formative assessment.

One aspect of instruction that typically engenders considerable student complaint is course exams. Students chafe under activities designed to document their mastery of course content. This explains part of their objection, but not all of it. Faculty also have little training in test construction and have been known to write bad exams. In some cases, this may be a persistent problem. Getting input from students about the nature of the problem from their perspective can be valuable. Instructors can do this by attaching to the exam a short evaluation form: "Grade the Exam" (McMullen-Pastrick and Gleason, 1986). This does not mean that students assign themselves the grade they would like to receive; rather, it gives them an opportunity to "grade" the exam in given categories such as its fairness, the clarity of the questions, the degree to which the exam met the students' expectations, the balance of different types of questions, the exam's effectiveness as a learning experience, and whatever else the instructor tries to accomplish with the exam. On an item such as the clarity of the questions, instructors can go so far as to ask students to list the questions they had no trouble understanding. This particular activity offers instructors a unique opportunity to identify with students. During the exam debriefing, discussion is not only about how the students did but how the exam fared as well.

Instructors can take the same sort of approach with the course readings. Instructors itemize on an instrument how they hope the reading assignments have been carried out, and students indicate the degree to which this occurred. The point here is not to cause instructors to despair — students in general do not complete reading assignments as instructors wish they would. Finding out how students do this is only the first step. In the second step, the individual instructor explores the alternatives with students and colleagues. How else can the reading assignments be designed or configured so that students will use them in a manner that is more consistent with the instructor's objectives?

Some focused topic instruments do exist, soliciting, for example, input about the lecture techniques of the instructor (University of London Teaching Methods Unit, 1976); discussion, laboratory, and studio experiences, respectively (Bergquist and Phillips, 1975a); and the classroom environment (Fraser, Treagust, and Dennis, 1986). Course material reviews that fall within the checklist/inventory category are also available (Weimer, 1987b) or can be created. Most focused topic instruments will probably have to be created because few exist in the literature. This can be beneficial in that faculty members learn from constructing the instruments.

To make an instrument, one must clearly identify the ingredients or the aspect of instruction one wants to assess and follow that with some sort of description of how that aspect or those component parts are supposed to work. "Did the items on the exam fairly represent the emphasis they were given in the class and text?" The activity cannot help but make the instructor much more conscious of the role this aspect of instruction plays in the larger instructional scheme of the course.

Virtually any aspect of instruction can be the topic of a focused instrument and probably will benefit from the close and exclusive attention so long as the instructor understands that every aspect of instruction is to some degree affected and influenced by all other aspects. To wrench them out of the course context and examine how they function in isolation skews the perspective. At some point, they must be put back in the picture and viewed from a distance.

Using focused topic instruments is generally not the first step in developing instructional awareness. Such instruments are usually more effective after some broader formative activities have occurred — after the instructor has identified some general areas in which improvement efforts will focus. Focused topic instruments are useful in acquiring the extra or more detailed information that might be helpful in unraveling contradictory or confounding conclusions that emerged in other evaluation results. Finally, focused topic instruments can be used to solicit input on the effectiveness of specific alterations that have been implemented. If an instructor is taking a whole new tack with homework assignments or exams or lecture organization, he or she can and should solicit specific input as to the effectiveness of the changes. This type of instrument is especially well suited to accomplish these objectives.

Summary

Formative feedback instruments do not automatically improve teaching. College teachers must use them in appropriate ways to achieve that objective. This chapter has reviewed the nature of the relationship between the evaluation and improvement of instruction, proposed certain logistical and procedural guidelines to increase the contributions of formative feedback, and reviewed a variety of instrument formats and types that one can use as part of the process of acquiring input that will improve instruction. The potential contributions of formative feedback acquired via instruments is great, but this is only the first of several ways to gather information that can increase the quality of college teaching.

5

✦✦✦✦✦✦✦✦✦✦✦✦✦✦✦✦✦✦✦✦✦✦✦✦✦✦

A Flexible Mix
of Improvement Activities

THIS CHAPTER considers a variety of ways, other than through the written methods described in Chapter Four, in which instruction can be positively affected. These activities include reading, videotaping and microteaching, dialogue (in several different forms), instructional observation, feedback activities with students, and the use of instructional grants. Even this brief list of activities shows their wide diversity. About all they have in common is that each involves some action — something that instructors do — and each activity in some way focuses the instructor's attention on teaching.

How do these activities improve instruction? Consider the question in light of the improvement process proposed. The activities contribute to various steps in the process. Reading certainly helps to develop instructional awareness, as does reviewing a videotaped teaching sample. Virtually all the activities offer input useful in the elaboration and refinement of one's sense of the instructional self. When it comes to making change choices, the instructional observation of others makes a contribution, as does dialogue in its several forms. In fact, the more information about teaching, the more ideas, strategies, and approaches encountered, the more informed the change choices will be. Implementing changes can sometimes be facilitated by a microteaching experience, certainly by an instructional grant. Instructional observation by a colleague and feedback activities with students can contribute to the reassessment step in the process. Some of the activities can do double or triple duty in the process, depending on the specific focus of the activity undertaken. Unlike the written input provided by instruments, which contributes most directly to step two in the process, these other activities relate to each step in the process.

In addition to having the potential to contribute to the improvement process, these activities have other advantages that relate to overcoming barriers and increasing motivation. Many of the activities are innovative, a bit novel, and so confront faculty with ideas and information about teaching that spark thought, reaction, and change in the classroom. This can be exciting, especially for faculty members who may have been teaching for some time without much excitement. Moreover, these activities are adaptable, able to be configured so that they represent the instructional needs and interests of the individual faculty member, a fact that has motivational implications. It is now widely acknowledged that students learn differently. It seems equally appropriate to consider alternative ways of learning about teaching, ways that might respond to the different learning styles and strategies of faculty. Finally, because participation in many of these activities offers input in a general and objective way—unlike evaluations with results that are sometimes too close for comfort—faculty respond less defensively and more constructively.

Before moving to the activities, we need to keep two caveats in mind. Many faculty members who have participated in some of these activities find them "fun." They like doing them, which sounds just fine to those of us working with them on instructional improvement. The first caveat relates to the quick-fix, instant-cure problem addressed in Chapter Three: There are no easy answers to better teaching. So while faculty may be having "fun" with an activity, they cannot "play" their way to better teaching. These activities like all other improvement efforts require work, effort, and dedication. It is true some of them can be done halfway or halfheartedly, but the benefits will be equally reduced in size and scope.

Second caveat: Although the activities included in this chapter are good, practical, efficient, and generally can be done economically, they are not necessarily the only, the right, or even the best activities in any definitive sense. The intention is that the chapter serve as a springboard, launching those of us committed to helping faculty members improve to consider still other activities with a potential to impact instruction positively.

Reading

At first glance, reading hardly seems to qualify as an innovative activity engendering enthusiastic faculty response. Upon closer examination, however, reading shows itself to be an improvement activity with considerable potential and sizable assets that other strategies cannot claim. Reading is easy (though not in the sense of requiring no work) because faculty members already read regularly and learn from printed materials. For most, the habit is well established. Moreover, reading is convenient; it requires no high-tech accoutrements and no strategic reordering of priorities. Best of all for many institutions and instructional development programs, reading is economical, especially when compared to other improvement activities.

Yet faculty rarely use reading as an improvement strategy, probably because appropriate reading materials are not well known or readily available. Only one journal, *College Teaching,* devotes itself exclusively to an interdisciplinary consideration of instruction at the postsecondary level. Most of the larger academic fields have pedagogical journals such as *Physics Teacher, Engineering Education, Journal of Chemical Education, Teaching Sociology,* and *Communication Education,* to name a few, but frequently these publications suffer a second-class status. They do not compare favorably with the leading research journals of the various disciplines. They also suffer a certain narrowness of perspective, which causes them to present the problems of teaching physics, engineering, chemistry, or whatever as unique, not to be understood or commented on by those outside the discipline. Even a quick review of these publications shows how many concerns, issues, and even answers they share. Teaching is the one activity professors from all fields have in common. It is unfortunate that consideration of it follows traditional academic boundaries.

Despite these problems, reading to improve instruction can be strongly recommended to faculty. Excellent books and articles do exist. They are located in a variety of publications, and faculty members who search them out will find themselves in places in the library they have never been before. Those who use reading as a means to improve their instruction quickly learn that much of the time they have to devote to the strategy is consumed by tracking down the resources. Authors in pedagogical journals rarely reference authors in other pedagogical journals, and very few attempts to prepare cross-disciplinary bibliographies occur. Moreover, some of the most valuable resources are not published in the typical book/journal format; for example, the Jossey-Bass New Directions for Teaching and Learning series, the Kansas State University IDEA Paper series, and the National Institute for Staff and Organizational Development Innovation Abstracts.

The difficulty an individual faculty member might have tracking down materials can be alleviated, if not eliminated, however, if an institution or those working to improve instruction within an institution devote some time and modest resources to assembling materials on teaching and learning that faculty members can more easily access. Pedagogical publications can be collected in one part of the library or in a faculty resource room — or even a bibliography of pedagogical journals available in the institution's library can be prepared and distributed.

The key question for many is whether or not faculty members will use the materials an institution might collect and assemble. Although no published data exist, the author's experience at Penn State justifies an emphatic yes, provided the institution takes a proactive stance in bringing these materials to the faculty's attention. Two or three short, useful, and readable reprints are offered each month in our instructional development newsletter. Faculty call and request single copies of the materials of interest to them. For the past five years, we have distributed an average of about 2,000 articles a year in response to faculty requests. We also prepare a variety of bibliographies on topics of interest to most teachers, such as increasing class participation, for example, which we distribute through the newsletter and during workshop programs. To each bibliography is attached an order form that faculty may fill out, indicating articles of interest they would like to receive. The Instructional Development Program supplies single copies in response to these requests. The same sort of activities can occur at an institution without an instructional development unit. Whoever has the task of encouraging instructional improvement should devote time to reading and begin assembling these materials, which can be made available or distributed by means of a variety of different mechanisms. For example, a dean or department head can reproduce materials of interest and place several copies on tables in the faculty dining room.

Our experience in distributing material to faculty members has taught us several lessons that might be valuable to others interested in using this strategy. Faculty find research results of interest only if they do not have to decipher them. Methodologies used to study teaching-learning variables are complicated and not easily understood by people outside the field. Those distributing research results to instructors need to translate findings, using language free from jargon and technical references.

Most important, faculty are interested in what they should or could *do* about the research results. What are the instructional implications? Researchers sometimes (and justifiably so) point out that results are not always definitive and/or generalizable, but if advice or suggestions can be offered, they ought to be included. Carrier (1983) in a review of research on student note taking provides an excellent illustration of how research results can be translated into practical instructional ideas. Nonetheless, a word of caution is in order. Research literature does not often concern itself with instructional implications. Researchers tend to report on research results in ways designed to influence further research, not practice. One is tempted to argue that this is not as it should be, but that is not really the issue. Those reviewing research results may find that they have to go out on a limb and suggest to faculty what they might consider doing as a consequence of certain findings.

When offering faculty members instructional materials to read, one must bear in mind that they are busy people — and probably not reading pedagogical material regularly because this feels like one more thing they must make time to do. It may be that a twenty-page article is better than a five-page treatment, but not if faculty members only have fifteen minutes during lunch to devote to reading. One of the most productive activities we completed at Penn State was to imagine what we would recommend if we could get faculty members to read ten articles on teaching. That evolved into our first "essential sources" bibliography (Gleason, 1984), which has been followed by other bibliographies and updates of the original version (Weimer, 1988). Faculty (like other people) can be enticed by audacity. Who else in academe boldly asserts that a bibliography contains the ten "best" of anything. Surprisingly enough, we have received very few objections to our offerings.

But does reading improve teaching? To date research has not inquired into the effectiveness of this strategy. However, the lack of research results does not prevent the proposing of hypotheses — reasons how and why reading might positively affect instructional quality. For example, reading can aid improvement efforts by infusing teaching with new ideas, important alternatives for faculty members to consider as they contemplate change choices. For example, suppose that there is some evidence that student participation in class is not what it should be. The question of how to increase classroom interaction stumps many faculty members, but a practical, no-nonsense approach such as that taken by Frederick (1981) in "The Dreaded Discussion: Ten Ways to Start" or the packed four-page analysis of the Kansas State University IDEA Paper (Hyman, 1982) "Questioning in the College Classroom" offers faculty all sorts of concrete activities to try. Sometimes the infusion is less concrete and more theoretical. Articles such as Fox's "Personal Theories of Teaching" (1983) and Eisner's "The Art and Craft of Teaching" (1983) bring faculty up against their own assumptions about teaching and learning and force them to consider how their beliefs about instruction get translated into classroom policies and practices.

Reading also forces faculty to reflect on their own instructional practices, and as a consequence it fosters the instructional awareness so essential to the improvement process. "Do I do that?" a college teacher wonders after reading a condensation and translation (such as Weimer, 1987d) of research findings (such as Barnes, 1983) on faculty questioning in the classroom. The next day finds that teacher more aware of questioning sequences that occur during class.

Finally, reading can inspire faculty members. Scholarly brows may be raised at the notion, but for too long the emotionally draining aspects of instruction have been overlooked or ignored. Yes, teachers do need to be inspired. Effective instruction requires teachers to give, often more than they get. Sometimes they give in institutional climates where the magnitude of what they contribute is not openly appreciated. As a result, most faculty members teach on, in increasingly challenging situations, without so much as a token acknowledgment of their efforts to meet those challenges. What they do is "expected," and they feel taken for granted. In the absence of such encouragement from above, or even with it, faculty will get a much needed boost when they read descriptions of teaching such as those provided by Hill in "Scaling the Heights" (1980), Ayers in "Thinking About Teachers and the Curriculum" (1986), and Franzwa in "Socrates Never Had Days Like This" (1984).

Of course, unless what is read gets translated into practice, reading will have little effect on instructional quality. What can those promoting this strategy do that might encourage faculty to take the important step from theory to practice? First, they can point out this very fact, always asking faculty members what they plan to do about whatever it is they have just read. Second, by making sure that faculty understand that like exercise, where an occasional workout is of limited value, reading too needs to be regular and systematic. It should be thought of as an ongoing part of preparing to teach. The notion of systematic implies that the analysis of the reading material needs to be critical, thoughtful, reflective. That need not preclude reading an inquiry such as Rigden's "The Art of Great Science" (1983) by the fireplace with a glass of wine in hand, but pedagogical reading needs to be thought of as bonafide scholarly development. When reading is so considered and the investment of time made, the need to do something about the reading is reinforced. Finally, reading can be incorporated in other activities designed to focus on the pragmatics of what has been read. Faculty members should be encouraged to discuss what they read, with each other or with whoever recommended the reading to them. Part of that discussion should focus on how the reading can be translated into instructional practices.

For all these reasons, reading deserves consideration as a legitimate instructional improvement strategy. For faculty members who may be independent learners, who may wish to direct attention to their teaching quietly and privately, or who may need an infusion of new ideas, reading can be an effective means of increasing classroom effectiveness.

Videotaping and Microteaching

Today's technology makes it very easy to record on videotape a sample of an instructor's teaching. Without the aid of any technology at all, instructors can do some form of "practice" teaching either for colleagues or whoever happens to be working with them. Such microteaching demonstrates the strategies and techniques the instructor seeks to use in the classroom. Empirical evidence is available to support the special effectiveness of both videotaping (Sharp, 1981) and microteaching (Levinson-Rose and Menges, 1981) in helping faculty members implement new strategies and techniques.

The problem for practitioners is a much more fundamental one: persuading faculty members to engage in videotaping or microteaching. Teachers and many other people find videotaping anxiety provoking (Fuller and Manning, 1973). The camera is a new and disturbing presence in the classroom and a confrontation with the self on tape is so total, so nakedly honest, that it can take one's breath away. The thought of teaching for the express purpose of having that teaching analyzed also paralyzes many faculty members. Thus, as effective as these techniques may be, their potential remains virtually untapped.

However, there are ways in which videotaping, particularly, can be used to encourage faculty exploration of this improvement strategy. Not all instructors are unduly inhibited by the videotaping experience and will, with only modest persuading, allow their tapes to be viewed by others. As a result, a library of videotaped teaching samples can be assembled for use by other instructors. Viewing the tapes benefits faculty members in several ways. Because the videotape is a fixed record of the teaching, any portion of it can be looked at more than once. This helps faculty to view teaching descriptively, not judgmentally. That is, one can show them how individual behaviors fit together to create a particular effect. They learn how a set of behaviors can affect different viewers in different ways. Even if a particular faculty member decides not to be taped, videotaping makes a valuable contribution to the development of the instructional awareness that he or she needs to understand and change certain teaching practices. In fact, viewing other people on tape often persuades faculty members to be taped themselves. They see how much they are likely to learn about their teaching and are then willing to cope with the anxiety the taping provokes.

That anxiety can be quelled still further if certain guidelines are adopted. For example, the instructional developer, department head, or any other conceivable "expert" should *not* do the taping. Rather, a student or other neutral party, possibly someone from the instructional media center, should do it. The tape becomes the exclusive property of the faculty member from the moment the recording ends until he is finished with it. This means the faculty member decides exactly what happens with the tape. If he wants to look at it alone and then erase it, fine. If he wants to share it with a colleague or instructional developer after having seen it alone first, fine. If he wants the outside viewer to watch the tape and provide written feedback, fine. If he wants to watch the tape with the outside viewer and share reactions verbally, fine. What happens to the tape is at the faculty member's discretion totally.

However, that does not mean that all ways of reviewing videotaped teaching samples are equally beneficial. Those helping instructors use the strategy should offer them information that will help them make informed choices. Research (Fuller and Manning, 1973) has shown that when people see themselves on tape, they tend to focus on the physical: "Do I look that old?

Where did I get that tie? My hair's too long." That kind of feedback may motivate change but not the kind that is going to improve instruction. Moreover, the personal involvement of the teacher sometimes prevents him or her from seeing behaviors that may be very obvious to others. For example, the author and others once reviewed a tape of an instructor who rocked from side to side throughout the whole lecture. When he discussed his reactions to the tape with us, he never mentioned the rocking. When we asked him about it, he looked as though he did not understand what we were saying. When we reviewed the tape with him, he was surprised and astounded that he could have missed such a noticeable feature of his teaching.

Obviously, then, if faculty members are going to view the tape alone, they need to be counseled about their tendency to focus on the physical. One way of doing this is to tell them to play the tape and look at themselves, then rewind the tape and look at the teaching. Faculty can also benefit from using a checklist or other instrument that directs their attention to certain behaviors at certain times (a sample appears in Centra, 1979, pp. 86–89). Checklists work to focus the feedback and force the viewer using them to look at specific aspects of the teaching performance. Videotaped teaching samples can be used to help faculty members see how a checklist directs their attention to specific aspects of the teaching. In this way, faculty members learn a bit about looking at tapes before viewing their own.

However, a better way to view a videotaped teaching sample is with someone else. This does not necessarily imply simultaneous viewing, but faculty reactions need the perspective and objectivity an outsider (colleague or instructional developer) can provide. In addition, the outsider is more likely to see things the faculty member (even one with a checklist in hand) missed and respond to specific behaviors in different ways than the faculty member. The instructor who has been taped needs to be in charge of selecting who does the viewing, but those selected must understand that they are not trained and in most cases not experienced viewers of instruction. They have lots to learn about how to observe and describe the teaching that they see. Chapter Six is helpful in this regard.

Probably the most successful strategy for faculty members interested in using videotaping is to pair them up with each other. Two people watch a videotaped sample, fill out a checklist, and discuss with each other what they have seen and how they feel about it. Then they have their own teaching taped, watch each other's tapes, and meet to review both tapes and share their reactions with each other. Their discussions will be most successful if they simply point out behaviors and how those behaviors made them feel. In other words, the discussions should be descriptive, not judgmental, giving each participant a clear and vivid view of the teaching observed.

Much of the same advice applies to microteaching. Those offering feedback on the sample instruction need to focus on behaviors — what the instructor did during the presentation. The question for the faculty member involved is one of representativeness. To what extent was the teaching influenced by the artificiality of the microteaching setting? Is this how the instructor "normally" teaches? A classic answer appeared at the end of a videotape the author once reviewed. Class had ended and students were beginning to file out. One student rushed through the crowd, stood directly in front of the camera and pulled out a penciled note: "This instructor has never been this good before." The student may or may not have been right, but the point he made is that observers of teaching (be they animate or inanimate) affect the teaching.

Sometimes the anxiety and exhibitory nature of the microteaching setting can be modified by a slight change of focus. For example, Leder, Jones, Paget, and Stillwell (1987, p. 186) report a version of microteaching in which the objective was an increased understanding of good teaching practices generally as they applied to the whole field of mathematics. Two volunteer math instructors were asked to prepare and teach two one-hour sessions on a topic "suitable for mature, educationally sophisticated but relatively naive learners of mathematics," in other words, a group of colleagues not from the math department. These "students" were encouraged to take notes on the content as well as to identify what, if anything, was making the subject difficult and what could be done to make the content clearer. Subsequent discussions explored responses to these questions at length, in terms of how they related to the instruction observed and what that implied about instruction throughout the discipline. In this case the value of the microteaching experience extends to many others besides the instructor providing the teaching sample. For the instructor involved, the anxiety no doubt still existed, but the activity fulfilled a much larger and less personal purpose.

Videotaping and microteaching do have the potential to make a positive impact on instructional quality. They deserve a place among instructional development techniques and strategies that can be recommended to faculty members.

Dialogue

The generic term *dialogue* reflects the wide range of interactive activities that the instructional improver can propose as means of encouraging attention to better teaching. The activities suggested in this section lie along a continuum beginning with seminars and workshops, moving to specific and general discussions, and ending with private exchanges between colleagues. They share the same continuum in that each utilizes verbal exchange to inform and influence instructional practice.

The value of this strategy lies in its ability to encourage still more talk about teaching, a subject infrequently discussed by academics. Gaff (1978, p. 53) reported more than ten years ago that in a survey of 1,680 faculty from fourteen institutions, "42 percent reported that never during their entire career had anyone talked with [them] in detail about [their] teaching and helped [them] to clarify [their] course objectives, devise effective student evaluation, or develop a more effective approach for certain kinds of students. Only 25 percent said this had happened more than twice." One hopes those figures might have increased by now, but on many of the large research campuses, they probably have not.

Dialogue about teaching does effectively and usually unobtrusively contribute to the improvement process. It helps to develop instructional awareness. The ideas and input of others contribute to that elaborated understanding of the instructional self. Faculty members can be very motivational to each other, often empowering each other to implement changes and helping with the assessment of those new policies and practices.

Faculty frequently find the exchanges comforting. They discover that student passivity and lack of interest, for example, are not unique to their own classes, but in fact reflect problems that plague classes across campus. If faculty can be encouraged to talk about teaching with colleagues in other disciplines, they quickly discover that they can learn important lessons from each other. Granted, physics is not taught like English, but the physicist may well use techniques applicable in the English classroom. The point is simple: The instructional challenges that all college teachers share are far greater than the pedagogical proclivities of their individual disciplines. Regular and frequent cross-disciplinary dialogue about teaching makes sizable contributions to the creation of an overall climate conducive to instructional health and well-being. It is mentioned again in Chapter Seven on the role of academic leaders in creating that kind of climate.

The character of the dialogue is an important determinant of its success. Talk about teaching tends to have three characteristics: It is highly judgmental ("Oh, she's the best teacher we have in this department."), discusses aspects of teaching abstractly ("His teaching is very disorganized."), and offers broad generalizations ("She's terrific with students."). If the purpose of the dialogue is to help an instructor teach more effectively, such comments must be accorded low marks and avoided wherever possible.

Seminars and Workshops. Teaching effectiveness workshops were among the first activities used in current faculty development efforts. They still rank among the most popular. A recent review of the literature on faculty and organizational development (Bland and Schmitz, 1988) identified forty-nine different strategies designed to develop faculties, departments, and institutions. Of the 287 published works describing those strategies, 78 discuss workshops, making them the most mentioned strategy. The most popular and most effective, however, are not always the same. Seminars and workshops do have assets and liabilities. For example, if they are done well, if the presenter is effective and the publicity positive, they do much to raise consciousness. They make faculty members aware of the issues and can be very motivational. On the other hand, seminars sometimes function a bit like revival services. People get converted and teach with renewed passion and vigor for the next few days, but two weeks later, the old patterns and habits have reasserted themselves. Unless workshops and seminars are designed to involve participants and include follow-up activities, they have limited impact on the sustained behavior changes needed to alter teaching practices permanently.

Moreover, also like camp meetings, some people attend regularly but others never do. This is an inherent liability only if workshops are the sole improvement strategy being used. But even if the objective is only to raise consciousness, planners must recognize that some instructors will not be present to have theirs lifted.

Workshop successes seem particularly dependent on two variables: the presenter and the topic. Sometimes an outside expert with a "national" reputation can be a drawing card, but not as often as one might expect. Faculty members unfamiliar with pedagogical literature and trends are not likely to know the experts, and so unless the person gives a credible performance, they may not be particularly impressed. There are some advantages in using local talent. Such people will be around after the presentation and can encourage subsequent interaction. Local faculty members should not be presented as "experts" invited to tell everybody else how to teach. They should be billed as colleagues with ideas and information to be discussed for the purpose of fostering further exploration of and dialogue on the issues. Local college teachers can be assembled in panels to discuss issues from different perspectives. For example, at the beginning of the year at Penn State, we have success with a panel of faculty members addressing new faculty appointees on "Teaching and Research: The Delicate Act of Balancing Both." We balance the panel with two comparatively new faculty members (people in their second and fourth year at the institution), one who has just successfully acquired tenure, and an old-timer to give the topic a total career perspective. The new appointees seem especially interested in panel responses to the query "What advice do I wish somebody had given me when I first arrived at this institution?"

But panels are not successful automatically. Some members may dominate and others may get defensive, both of which identify the need to work with panelists before a presentation. On one occasion we assembled a panel of the university's best teachers, asking them to share some of the secrets of their success. Most somewhat apologetically announced that they had no secrets, did not do anything particularly noteworthy, and were in the dark themselves when it came to accounting for their success in the classroom. We learned that being a good teacher and knowing why teaching strategies work are two separate skills.

Topics also add to the success of workshops. Issues ought to be timely. Faculty members today are interested in ways to overcome student passivity, especially ways to get students to participate in class and ways to encourage students to think. Though not especially well informed on the topic, most faculty members find the recent research on learning styles and cognitive processing of interest, especially if the session focuses on instructional implications such as those identified by Svinicki and Dixon (1987). Most instructors find large classes very challenging, and a special topic session addressing that issue will bring out all sorts of people, many of whom may not appear during regular sessions. Lacey (1988, p. 65) recommends sessions that meet "practical needs and can result in tangible changes in the way faculty teach" as opposed to sessions that address very broad questions. He offers as examples workshops on using computers in teaching and teaching writing across the curriculum.

With workshops and seminars, organizers should try innovative approaches. A workshop series that joins faculty and students in dialogue on topics of mutual interest — for example, "getting grades versus getting learning," "general education versus required courses," and "academic integrity versus academic dishonesty"—can be very successful. The workshop format should begin with faculty members and students briefly sharing their respective positions on and interest in the issue. Attendees are then organized into small groups with equal numbers of faculty and student members. They discuss a series of questions and then return to the large group for further exploration of the issues. The sessions can be especially successful in showing students and faculty each other's perspective. That kind of dialogue is difficult to cultivate in a classroom, where the almighty grade often makes its obtrusive presence known.

The assumption that faculty members need input from others as an essential component of efforts to improve warrants the conclusion that workshops and seminars ought to be structured so that they include some opportunity for exchange and discussion. For the same reasons that students learn better if they are involved and active participants, faculty too need to be more than passive receivers of instructional information. This makes workshops superior to seminars, in most cases. The impact of the seminar or workshop can be heightened by incorporating follow-up activities as part of the program design. And because improvement efforts are under the aegis and control of the faculty members involved, attendance at workshops and seminars should not be mandatory. Additional suggestions for successful workshops are offered by Browne and Keeley (1988).

Discussion Groups. Because dialogue contributes insights and information to improvement efforts, faculty members can be encouraged to discuss instructional issues in groups. Generally, the dialogue works better if the discussion topics are focused and the interaction sustained, meaning that the group meets more than once.

Topics can be focused and groups assembled in all sorts of ways. Lists of potential topics (for example, motivation, grading policies and practices, academic integrity, use of group projects) can be circulated to the faculty. Members indicating interest in a particular topic can be convened as a group. Or potential participants can be invited directly. New faculty members or those teaching required courses or those teaching upper-division seminars can be invited to join a group discussing topics relevant to the shared instructional situation. Group size should be small so that all members have the opportunity to participate fully.

Because faculty have much to learn from teachers in other disciplines, organizers should form groups across academic boundaries unless teachers in the same department specifically request to meet together. In addition to providing an opportunity to learn from others, cross-disciplinary groups offer several other advantages. Often faculty members within a department know each other well. They have exchanged ideas and opinions on many issues during many meetings. Because they know each other so well, they tend to "listen" already knowing what another will say. In a new group, even old opinions and ideas sound fresh. Finally, if a faculty member is experiencing some difficulty and wishes to seek the counsel of colleagues, that will occur much more readily outside the department. After all, it is peers from the department who are called on first to pass judgment on each other. When the interdisciplinary group convenes, let members set the agenda in terms of further refining the topic and suggesting the number of subsequent meetings. If an instructional development program or unit is sponsoring the sessions, that unit can handle the logistics, arranging meeting places and sending reminder notices.

Faculty discussions do need to be informed and focused. College teachers' time is too precious to use for the purpose of pooling ignorance, and one of the themes of this book is that on instructional issues teachers are not as informed as they ought to be. So unless resources are identified, collected, and somehow shared with the group, faculty members will end up exchanging a good deal of misinformation.

In focused discussions, the group convenes to consider a particular topic and confines the discussion to an exploration of that issue. Discussions do, by their very nature, tend to digress and wander off the topic being considered. However, if the advertisement says that the group will exchange ideas on handling the logistics of large classes (office hours, makeup exams, handing out material, and so on) and that only happens tangentially, participants will resolve the problem by not attending the next group meeting. This does not mean that discussion groups must have an "official" leader; it does mean that someone needs to assume responsibility for keeping the group on track, focused on the topic at hand.

Although discussions do work best, in terms of their impact on teaching, if the group tackles an issue comprehensively, less thorough considerations are not without value. If the force convening the group is a department head, a small instructional development unit, or an individual faculty member who does not have a collection of resources to offer the group, even a single article of interest (for example, "The Effects of Exam Anxiety on Grandma's Health," Chiodo, 1986) can be used to facilitate a valuable exchange. The article can be circulated (Chiodo's is only a page) and interested faculty members invited to meet for a lunchtime discussion. One group of interested faculty members met on a more or less regular basis for better than a year using this model. Whenever a group member read something of instructional interest, he or she circulated it and proposed a date for discussion. Those who were interested and could attend, did.

If discussion groups are to function as an improvement strategy, several precautions are in order. Faculty members on many campuses are "committed" to death, and the thought of yet another meeting may not be a particularly pleasing proposition. Yet these are not run-of-the-mill committee meetings with externally set agendas. They are guided conversations exploring instructional issues of relevance and importance to college teachers. Some people avoid groups because committees do work in circuitous ways and more often than not come up with camels when horses are needed. Again, those convening the group are well advised to devote time to describing the aims and purposes of the discussions as well as suggesting appropriate group protocol. Faculty comments should be kept concise. People who need to should control the number of comments they make. The opinions of others should be respected. These groups need not resolve disputed issues. Discussion should be kept practical: What can be done about this in class tomorrow? They should also be positive, not permitted to degenerate into gripe sessions. The objective of such procedural protocols is not to stifle discussion but to establish a climate in which the participants can learn and grow.

Because groups, especially committees, tend to have less than positive associations for many people, those advocating them as an instructional improvement strategy may have to devote considerable effort to "selling" faculty members on the idea. Advocates will also need to work to structure and guide sessions so that counterproductive group behavior does not undermine the objectives. Faculty members who themselves have benefited from instructional discussions are often the best advocates for this strategy. In many cases, they can be prevailed upon to facilitate and guide new groups. This tactic works well to ensure that they continue learning about teaching and that faculty new to instructional discussions will have a positive experience.

Private Conversations. At the opposite end of the continuum from the public workshop sessions are the private exchanges, most often those occurring between colleagues. Not as much of this type of dialogue takes place as should. Faculty members seem more comfortable talking about research interests — probably because such conversations are grounded in knowledge of the content, where faculty expertise lies. Knowledge about teaching is more experiential and anecdotal, which tends to give it a second-class status. It supposedly lacks the substantive grist needed for true intellectual exchange. Such notions are unfortunate because they are untrue. Teaching is a highly complex phenomenon, some aspects of which are still poorly understood. It would benefit from the focused and rigorous attention sharp minds could give it. Faculty classroom competence would increase if college teachers better understood the complex interplay of variables that combine to create success in the classroom. Those who wish to use this strategy may have to begin by persuading faculty that private conversations have benefit. A specific illustration may be enough to prove the point. An excellent one is offered by Elbow (1980), who recounts an experience of observing and communicating with a fellow faculty member about the faculty member's teaching. The beauty of this strategy is that even though it frequently starts out as something one faculty member is doing to another, very quickly the doer feels the benefits in her or his own teaching.

Initially, private exchanges work best if the participants have something to talk about; maybe a shared instructional observation, mutual attendance at an instructional seminar, or joint review of a videotaped teaching sample. Usually, the specific experience functions to open a much broader discussion of teaching and learning issues. Thoughtful or provocative written materials can stimulate interaction between individuals as well. If an exchange has been profitable, then faculty are more receptive to free-flowing talks in which the exchange moves away from teaching generally to what the individual teacher does and believes specifically. At that point, a conversation agenda (Weimer, 1987a), which inquires as to teaching models, how instructors decide when the teaching has gone well, enduring effects, and who is to blame when a class goes bad, provides a useful protocol to guide larger and more disclosive exchanges about teaching.

Much of the success of private dialogue depends on the nature of the relationship that exists or develops between the two teachers. Issues pertaining to this matter are explored more fully in Chapter Six. However, if the dialogue proceeds from general to specific, from how other instructors do it to how "I" do it, the potential of this strategy to improve instruction may be unequalled. This sort of one-on-one consultation in the context of a trusting and validating relationship changes behavior in permanent and substantive ways. Notions of collegiality make such relationships possible. At present private conversations do not improve instruction very much because they rarely occur. Instructional climates at many institutions do not encourage and at some institutions even discourage such sustained and substantive instructional exchanges. The important role of administrators in creating environments that recognize and value scholarly dialogue about teaching cannot be overstated.

To conclude, the value of dialogue about teaching— whether it be dialogue organized to occur in seminars, workshops, and programs, dialogue structured to happen in small group exchanges, or dialogue between two people who share common instructional interests and concerns—has not yet received its due. If a recognition of that value can be cultivated by making sure that interactions are informed, relevant, and practical, instruction can and will improve as a result.

Instructional Observation

Actual observation of the teaching of others can also contribute significantly to efforts to improve. As with instructional evaluation, the topic has received considerable attention in recent years and has to some degree been complicated and compromised by the use of the strategy to generate information used in personnel decisions. Background information relevant to this summative use and some procedural issues important to the success of this strategy are discussed at length in Chapter Six. At this point, however, it is important to recognize the viability of observation as an improvement activity. In the context of this chapter it is appropriate to note and discuss the observations of others where the purpose is to improve the instruction of the *observer* rather than the teaching of the observed.

With the plethora of writings about observations to improve or establish the instructional competence of the observed, the value of observations to the observer has been virtually ignored. Yet, within the formative realm, where the ultimate objective might be to observe the instructor, having that instructor first observe someone else increases self-awareness and offers persuasive firsthand proof of the value of the strategy. Even if the person who has done the observing does not have the confidence to request an observation of herself, her exposure to the teaching strategies and techniques of others potentially enlightens and enriches her own teaching. Some specific examples illustrate how this works.

A kind of Cook's tour of classes can be arranged quite easily and economically. Faculty members with reputations as good teachers or faculty recipients of teaching awards might be asked to open their classrooms to visitors on certain predetermined and publicly specified days or to permit their classes to be on a list for a term with the proviso that visitors first call and arrange a time for their visit. Those setting up the tour may choose classes whose teachers use an instructional strategy well, not (necessarily) whose teachers are acknowledged experts. One instructor at Penn State does a superb job of integrating material from student panels into his course. We frequently send faculty members interested in more effectively incorporating student presentations to visit his class. Perhaps the Cook's tour one term focuses on different but effective use of discussion strategies, another term identifies faculty members who teach large classes well, and still another identifies examples of effective laboratory instruction. The cardinal rule for the Cook's tour is that faculty members are invited to have their classes on the tour; anyone's decision to decline is graciously respected. Those who accept specify the days for the visits, control the number of visitors, and may without excuse or question decline the request of a particular individual to visit.

If the Cook's tour idea is too formal and public for some, the same activity can occur at a much more informal level. The department head knows some good teachers in her department or others and asks them if a certain individual faculty member can be encouraged to attend their classes. Instructional development units are in an especially good position to link observers to classes in which they might observe something of interest and value. Quite accidentally, those of us working in the Instructional Development Program at Penn State once derived an unexpected benefit when we asked a faculty member, who had been working diligently with us on incorporating a number of new activities into an old course, if we could send her a visitor. She responded to the request almost ecstatically: "You mean you think I'm good enough for other people to learn from?" It seemed like an amazing statement for someone in the education business, but we understood the intent and could honestly say yes. She later said our request had given her morale a great boost.

Instructional observations are especially beneficial for faculty members new to college teaching. At the beginning of a teaching career the need for models, ideas, and ways of handling the mechanics of teaching can be almost overwhelming. The opportunity to view others' teaching, from a teacher (no longer a student) perspective, can be extremely helpful. Observations of this kind are also valuable when the objective is to stimulate private exchanges between colleagues. Have two faculty members visit somebody else's class — preferably in a discipline not their own. (As already discussed, when chemists, engineers, philosophers, and so on view their own brand of teaching, they focus almost exclusively on the content.) They can either attend the same class or different classes. During the conversation that follows they discuss what they observed and how they responded to it. Generally, they run out of time long before they run out of topics. These observations can also increase the effectiveness of discussions between a faculty member and the consultant working with him or her on the improvement process. It is one thing to describe to the faculty member who has little interaction from students strategies and techniques that he or she can use to generate student participation. It is quite another thing to reinforce that description with a specific example of an instructor in action, using the strategies and acquiring the results.

Instructional observation occurs most naturally when the observer takes the course. Observers in that category are almost exclusively students enrolled in the course for credit. Faculty members rarely if ever take or even sit in on each other's classes out of genuine interest. How unfortunate. The benefits are extraordinary. Faculty members find out how it feels to be a student. That feeling tends to fade the longer the time spent in front of a class. They rediscover the frustration of learning new and unfamiliar content, especially if they venture into fields unlike their own. They experience the effects of different instructional strategies. Students and teachers benefit from the presence of an experienced and motivated learner in class. Why do faculty members avoid taking classes? A lack of time is part of the reason, but time is a negotiable variable. Units, segments, or even a few consecutive class sessions can be beneficial. Probably more pivotal in decisions to avoid classes are fears that attending them will somehow violate academic freedom, that faculty "students" have no right to be there. Certainly that conclusion is corroborated by institutional climates where what happens in classrooms always occurs behind closed doors.

Although the taking of courses as an improvement strategy will probably not be put into practice, it should not be forgotten. Moreover, persuasive examples of how a systematic use of this strategy can affect both teaching and learning do exist. Starling (1987, p. 3) writes vividly of his experiences in a program at a college in Florida where a faculty member joins a group of students to form a "community of learners." The faculty member is released from all teaching duties to take a full course load with twelve to fifteen students. The article summarizes an innovative approach to getting faculty members into the classroom, but far more compelling is Starling's description of his experiences: "The master-learner experience forced me to acknowledge that there is a clear causal connection between these two statements: (a) teachers get very little reliable feedback, and (b) being a student is 'a pain.' On certain days I couldn't wait to return to teaching to put my new knowledge to work; on other days, the prospect of trying to fix so much that was broken led me to consider less demanding professions."

Faculty members do not spend much time in each other's classrooms. If they can be persuaded to make even a few visits, they discover how much they have to learn about teaching generally and their own specifically. If those visits can occur in a climate of openness and trust, where the visit may just as often be for the benefit of the observer as for the observed, instructional observation can make sizable contributions to the improvement process.

Feedback Activities with Students

Chapter Four considered student input acquired via instructional evaluation instruments. The focus in this section is still on acquiring input with the potential to improve instruction, but the mechanisms described here do not involve any sort of paper and pencil instrumentation. Rather, they are activities that offer instructors and students unique opportunities to exchange information relevant to the experiences occurring in a specific class.

Quality Control Circles. When instructors use quality control circles, they call on a management technique (generally credited to the Japanese) that involves employees (in this case, students) in some of the decision-making activities of a company (in this case, a class). After the instructor has explained the activity to the class, a group of volunteers is assembled. The group meets regularly (sometimes weekly, sometimes biweekly, or once a month) with the instructor. During the meetings, the instructor solicits input from the group about how the class is going. Topics include such matters as the role of homework in the class — what do students think the homework is designed to accomplish, how much time are people spending on it, whether students believe it helps them on exams, whether the instructor should work some of the homework problems in class. Other sessions may be devoted to discussion of the exams, the pace and organization of lecture material, the instructor's use of questions in class, and so on. The instructor reports back to the class on meetings with the group, making special mention of any changes that he or she is implementing as a result of group input and encouraging students who may disagree with opinions expressed by the quality circle to let their views be known to members of the group. Some instructors announce meeting times of the circle so that any interested student can attend.

The success of the technique depends on the willingness of the instructor to listen to input from the group and to respond to information provided. That may mean making some changes in the way the class is run. Instructors who use the technique usually report that when they do make changes, the students who have recommended them have a vested interest in their outcome and as a result work with the instructor to ensure their success. In one sociology class, students suggested that the instructor talk less after showing films so that students would have a chance to share their reactions. After showing the next film, the instructor announced that on the basis of the advice of the circle she was asking for student responses before offering her own. What followed was the liveliest discussion of the term. When it lagged, members of the circle jumped in to maintain the momentum.

The technique seems especially well suited for obtaining input from large classes, where size precludes the possibility of personal relationships with students. Meeting regularly with a small group from a large class helps instructors keep their finger on the pulse of the class. Kogut (1984) confirms this conclusion in his published report of quality circle activities in large introductory chemistry courses.

Small Group Instructional Diagnosis (SGID). First used at the University of Washington (Redmond and Clark, 1982), small group instructional diagnosis (SGID) relies on a unique interview structure to solicit relevant student input about a class. Student reactions are then shared with the instructor. The approach, used in different variations (Bennett, 1987), basically works like this. At the beginning of the second half of a regular class period, the instructor introduces a "facilitator" (sometimes an instructional development specialist, sometimes a trained faculty member, or in our case at Penn State, a trained student) who, in the words of Bennett (1987, p. 101), "has come to gather ideas about the students' learning experiences" in the class. The course instructor leaves the class at this point. The students divide into small groups and are assigned to the task of responding to a series of questions soliciting input about their experiences so far. Sample questions appear in Redmond and Clark (1982) and Bennett (1987). After a period of discussion, the groups are asked to report back to the facilitator. Each group's opinions and conclusions are held up for verification and discussion by the entire class. After some discussion, the conclusions are recorded and then reported back to the instructor during a private meeting.

The approach is beneficial to all parties involved. The students have the opportunity to see whether their experiences and assessments are the same as those of their classmates, and they begin to understand what sort of a challenge confronts an instructor who is trying to provide sound learning experiences for students who have different learning needs and expectations. The facilitator can also help students develop the kind of instructional awareness that will enable them to understand experiences in other classes better and can help them learn to express criticisms of the teaching constructively.

The faculty member gets direct feedback from students without having to stand before the class and take it publicly. The presence of an intermediary gives the faculty member the distance necessary to put student reactions in context. The facilitator can also be helpful in identifying alternatives.

The technique is not without complications, however. Sometimes the logistics of schedules and available personnel are difficult to juggle. Facilitators must be trained. In one of our early experiences at Penn State, the facilitator (in this instance a faculty member) and the class got into a major argument, with the facilitator lecturing the students about their grade-grubbing attitude. The technique is new and different for students. They are unsure and hesitant to participate. They warm up to the idea slowly, finally generating useful responses in the last five minutes. We found the thirty-minute time frame too tight, but even then many instructors interested in the technique declined to participate because they could not "give up" thirty minutes of class time.

However, the technique is still a good one. Instructors gain valuable insights and are generally highly motivated to respond to student suggestions and critiques. The technique is an excellent way to open the door to further exchanges between instructor and students. In many cases, it gives instructors the confidence they need to stand before the class and request the same sort of feedback. Although face-to-face interactions between the instructor and students do not protect student anonymity, encouraging students to provide responsible input seems like a realistic educational objective.

Instructional Grants

Some institutions, generally under the auspices of an instructional development unit, competitively award faculty monies for the enhancement of a certain aspect or component of their instruction. Generally, the funds are directed toward a specific course and support activities such as developing supplementary materials, audiovisual illustrations, writing or computer components, or a new design for the course. Some of the funds provide support for faculty members wishing to develop new courses or cross-disciplinary or team-taught courses. Criteria for selecting projects for funding vary, but they often include the use of instructional innovations, the number of students affected by the project, and applicability to other courses in the curriculum. Sometimes the criteria change, one year emphasizing general education courses, another year curricular integration, and yet another instruction in classes enrolling more than 100 students. In most instances, fund recipients are expected to prepare reports of their project activities as well as evaluations of their effectiveness. At most institutions, this information is highlighted in some in-house publication or during a public display or report.

The activity appeals to many institutions because funds to support instructional projects can frequently be obtained from external sources, such as alumni and/or corporate gifts to the university. Moreover, even grants of modest size can have a dramatic effect on the instruction involved. Infusing a course with $2,000 can significantly change what transpires there. Do that for ten courses a year, and for a comparatively small expenditure, a sizable number of faculty members and students benefit. The grants do effectively improve instruction because they focus faculty attention on a particular course and make possible a series of changes not likely to happen otherwise. Faculty members tackle course challenges with renewed enthusiasm and vigor. Even though the focus may be on the content, the sense of energy frequently spills over, charging the teaching with new zest as well. Finally, grants work well because they allow instructors the independence and autonomy so important in successful academic work. Faculty members are responsible. They do this for themselves in ways of their own choosing, which dramatically affects their motivation and interest.

Summary

The activities described in this chapter make valuable contributions to the efforts of individuals and institutions to improve instruction. Their presence helps to create a climate that encourages instructional growth and development in very positive ways. They create the expectation of improvement and excellence in the classroom, while respecting instructional differences and diversity. As such, these activities are among the most versatile and valuable tools in the instructional improvement repertoire.

6

✦✦✦✦✦✦✦✦✦✦✦✦✦✦✦✦✦✦✦✦✦✦✦✦✦✦

Colleagues
Assisting Colleagues

COLLEAGUES can and should play a fundamental role in instructional improvement. Inherent in the academic understanding of what collegiality implies are notions of relationships in which shared experiences, interests, and concerns form strong bonds between professionals. Such relationships lend themselves to the discussion, analysis, and exploration of teaching and learning.

Despite this obvious potential, colleagues at most colleges and universities today contribute little to one another's instructional activities. They avoid each other's classrooms, believing that such visits border on violations of academic freedom and should only occur if they are required. Discussions of teaching tend to be nonspecific and general; rarely do they divulge the details of "what I do in class." Furthermore, colleagues regularly bemoan the lack of reward and recognition accorded teaching and bewail the lack of preparation evident in their students.

Yet some, like Edgerton (1988, p. 8), envision something better for their colleagues: "We must move to a culture in which peer review of teaching is as common as peer review of research . . . a culture in which professors ask their colleagues for comment on the syllabus of a course as routinely as they ask for comment on the prospectus for a book." That culture currently eludes us. This chapter aims to move it closer to our grasp. In working toward that objective, the chapter first considers colleagues as evaluators, then as reviewers, and finally as helpers.

111

Colleagues as Evaluators

Current policies and practices at many institutions do prescribe the involvement of colleagues in each other's teaching, but almost exclusively in the role of evaluators who pass judgment on each other's instructional effectiveness. In other words, the colleague contributes information that is used to make the personnel decisions that determine tenure, promotion, and often salaries. Too often, faculty members pass those judgments without their having been trained to teach, with little experience in observing instruction either inside or outside the department, without any institutionally or departmentally determined criteria against which to measure the instruction they are evaluating, and without having seen more than a couple of isolated samples of the teaching in question.

Faculty members acquire information on which to base their assessment of each other's teaching in a variety of different ways — many of them not particularly commendable. In the worst case scenario, hearsay spread among teachers, overheard comments from students, and discrete questions to advisees form the eclectic bases from which conclusions are drawn. An increasingly common and somewhat improved strategy uses in-class observations as the basis for judgment. However, peer instructional observations are particularly susceptible to problems when evaluators lack training, lack experience, do not use established criteria, and observe infrequently (Weimer, Kerns, and Parrett, 1988b). Because these characteristics describe peer reviewers at most college and universities today, problems result. These problems end up compromising the integrity of peer assessments and adversely affect faculty motivation and morale.

Consider first the technical problems associated with peer review — problems that worry researchers as they analyze data resulting from classroom observations. A succinct and simplified summary will suffice. The problems have been documented and elaborated by a variety of experts (Centra, 1979; Bergman, 1980; French-Lazovik, 1981; Doyle, 1983). These sources certainly should be consulted if observations by peers are used in promotion and tenure processes. The key problem involves the reliability of peer observations, the extent to which observers viewing the same teaching sample agree in their evaluation of an instructor. Quite simply peer observations are *not* very reliable. Faculty observers tend to disagree in their assessments — so much so that a number of the experts recommend against or strongly caution about using peer instructional observation data in promotion and tenure decisions.

Why do peers disagree? The researchers do not know for sure, but peers' lack of experience in making such observations, their lack of training, and the practices under which the observations occur seem likely culprits. Faculty who have not been trained to teach are not instructionally aware; they do not see the nuts and bolts, the bits and pieces that fit together into instructional processes. Faculty do not regularly observe each other's teaching; they have limited experience on which to fall back. Moreover, when they visit a class, their criteria for assessment are their own. The criteria may or may not be the same as those used by other colleague evaluators. Finally, the slice of instruction viewed is small: one day in one class. How representative is the sample? These background variables affect people's ability to "see" the instruction. Many of them have been shown to influence the quality of peer assessments at the secondary school level (McGreal, 1983).

The objections discussed so far, however, relate only to technical issues. Of more concern to the instructional improver are the impacts of summative peer assessments (in this case, specifically, classroom observations) on efforts to improve instruction. Quite bluntly, the impacts on morale and motivation are serious and so far almost universally negative. Consider two impacts: the anxiety associated with the peer assessments and the effectiveness of policies and practices associated with them in repressing dialogue about teaching. Begin by assuming the perspective of the faculty member (generally a younger and less experienced teacher) facing an observation by a senior member of the department. If the visit is announced, extra preparation is probably required (which also says something about the representativeness of the instruction observed), to say nothing of having to cope with the anxiety provoked by the impending visit. If the visit is unannounced, the visitor conducts a commando raid of sorts on the class, denying the teacher the opportunity to put the content and activities of the day into the larger context of the course. In this situation, the faculty member is forced to cope with the anxiety on the spot and in the presence of everybody in class. (This also has implications for the representativeness of the sample observed.)

Peer assessments very effectively repress dialogue about teaching in several different ways. First, there is the confidentiality associated with the peer evaluation. Faculty evaluators generally lobby hard to preserve confidentiality. It permits them to make far more "honest" assessments. In other words, they can make negative comments without having to communicate them to the faculty member involved. If the assessments are confidential, they cannot be discussed, thereby not only repressing but actually preventing dialogue. This adds further to the anxiety of the faculty member being observed, who finds out how well it went somewhere way down the road at the time the tenure decision is made public.

Some departments try to mitigate the effects of confidentiality by discussing the evaluations during the annual performance review or in a meeting after the teaching has been observed. But with the need to protect the confidentiality of the evaluation, the references to teaching tend to be oblique and veiled. Frequently important conclusions (especially negative ones) are omitted, and in general faculty members receive very little information of value when it comes to implementing changes. By virtue of conveying unclear, nonspecific, and incomplete information, such discussions also contribute to the devaluing of dialogue about teaching.

The whole process of summative peer review represses dialogue to the extent that faculty members being reviewed fear disclosure of instructional information that might be overheard, passed along, and ultimately used against them. How readily would an untenured faculty member divulge concerns and problems confronted in the classroom to a colleague who regularly sits on the department's promotion and tenure committee? It is much safer to respond to inquiries about how one's teaching is going by assuring the colleague who questions that it is going just fine.

If the assessments are discussed and evaluative letters are placed in the open section of the personnel file, the process still discourages constructive dialogue. The faculty member being evaluated is vulnerable. To argue is to jeopardize the quality of one's life within the academic community. Even if one is compelled to argue, the exchange seldom contributes positively to efforts to improve. Both parties are on the defensive, upholding long held beliefs about teaching, not listening to new ideas and insights.

Finally, summative peer assessments repress collegial dialogue because frequently the conclusions that are discussed are not communicated constructively. Here the vulnerability belongs not to the instructor but to the faculty member who is called in (often under duress) to do the evaluation and discuss the results. This vulnerability reflects the difficulty people have with communication situations where criticism must be conveyed face-to-face. Those problems are magnified when the exchange occurs with a peer and when the subject is the other person's teaching. The colleague offers criticism of an activity she or he may not do any better than the instructor observed. The colleague probably offers it without having considered the propriety of the criteria used to assess the teaching and after having seen only a small segment of a much larger performance. Finally, the colleague offers the criticism without much experience in having conveyed such criticism to others. As a result, conversations turn confrontational. Generalizations grow larger. Points are misunderstood or become personal. Feelings are hurt. After the exchange, talk about teaching diminishes while the conviction that peers do not contribute constructively to instructional improvement grows.

From many perspectives, this is the summative-formative dilemma of Chapter Four revisited. Obviously, summative evaluations have only limited improvement potential, if they have any at all. But the problem is even more serious than that. Many of the current practices of peer evaluation actually prevent colleagues from making any sort of formative contribution.

The evaluations themselves cannot be expected to do double duty and neither can the peers who make them. It is difficult to sit in judgment of a colleague's competence in the classroom and then encourage that instructor to divulge instructional problems and concerns.

Many who have written about colleagues as evaluators come to much the same conclusion. Cohen and McKeachie (1980), after a comprehensive review of research and literature on the topic, suggest using colleagues as integrators of information on teaching effectiveness and instructional consultants with strictly formative objectives. Scriven (1981, pp. 251–252), who asserts that classroom visits to evaluate teaching are not just "incorrect" but a "disgrace," sees visits by a consultant "to provide help to improve teaching" as being "defensible." Some argue against peer instructional observations because, in general, student and peer assessments of an individual instructor agree (Blackburn and Clark, 1975) and student evaluations do not suffer from the reliability problems (Marsh, 1984) that plague peer evaluations.

So far the picture painted for the contributions of colleagues as evaluators is bleak, perhaps overly so. Some faculty members and institutions do use instructional observations constructively. The technical and morale issues are not unsolvable (Weimer, Kerns, and Parrett, 1988b). Most institutions have not solved them, however, and do by their current policies and practices severely compromise the potential of colleagues to contribute to instructional improvement agendas. For those who wish to change current practices or carve out new roles for colleagues, the place to begin is with a review of the role of peers in the instructional evaluation activities of the institution. Careful attention ought to be given to the implication of those roles on efforts to encourage instructional improvement. Alternative roles for peers have been proposed and merit consideration.

Colleagues as Reviewers

Being colleagues does not necessarily "qualify" faculty to comment on each other's instruction. Because their qualifications to make summative instructional assessments have been called into question, what evidence might be offered to establish their qualifications when the objective is to help a colleague teach more effectively?

Consider four possible perspectives from which faculty may be "qualified" to review each other's instruction, independent of making definitive judgments about it. First, faculty members have behind them many long years as students. Moreover, most have not yet stopped learning. They know the experience of grappling with new ideas and information. When they talk to each other about teaching or visit each other's classrooms, they can and should do so from the perspective of a student or learner. This can help instructors understand what it may be like taking a particular course. They need to know when what they say in class is clear, understood, and sparking some interest and thought. Colleagues from outside the discipline are especially good at offering this perspective. Menges (1987, p. 86) explains why: "When feedback deals with teaching activities . . . a colleague's detailed knowledge of course content may hinder rather than help. Conversations tend to focus on substantive details which are less pertinent than data about teacher or student behavior."

Second, colleagues do not take each other's courses for credit, which affords them a certain objectivity students may not be able to summon. Even if instructors are very open, very solicitous of student input, there is always the risk that students are saying what they think they should say about the course in order to get the grade they would very much like to have. Colleagues, on the other hand, can see the course in terms of the educational experience it provides students; they can help an instructor sort through the vested student interests and see implications of instructional decisions in a larger, more objective context.

Third, colleagues have firsthand knowledge of an intimate experience with teaching. Most were in class yesterday. They know the bittersweet taste of teaching. The qualification here may be no more than the ability to empathize, but that value should not be underestimated. Instructors need to be able to tell a sympathetic listener about the student who turned on his Walkman during a recent lecture. They need to see a colleague respond with the same dismay and disgust they felt. College teachers need to know that other college teachers have similar joys and sorrows.

Finally, colleagues with knowledge of the discipline can claim the fourth qualification. Up to this point, the argument made about knowledge of the content has been that it can be detrimental; in some situations, however, it does help. When knowledge of the content makes a contribution to improvement efforts, it is knowledge of the material from a general rather than specific perspective. Colleagues do not contribute to each other's efforts to improve if they are arguing about when quantum numbers ought to be taught in the course. Yet understanding quantum numbers does make it easier to decide if they should be taught by discussion, by problem solving, by experiment, by homework assignments, or by any combination of the above. The way content is "shaped and ordered" by the various disciplines does have instructional implications, and colleague understanding of those content configurations can contribute to certain kinds of instructional decisions.

Colleague reviewers do have qualifications that students do not, qualifications that position them well to contribute to the improvement process proposed. A colleague reviewer who assumes the four perspectives outlined can help a faculty member acquire the objective input he or she needs to develop a more elaborate and accurate understanding of how he or she teaches. The colleague's advice as to alternatives will be better because these perspectives encourage the colleague to describe rather than judge teaching. The four perspectives also put the colleague in a good position to assess any alterations that the faculty member has implemented.

Colleagues as Helpers

To this point, with instructional improvement as the agenda, the role of colleagues as evaluators has been discouraged and the role of colleagues as reviewers encouraged. In this final section of the chapter, the reviewer role will be elaborated upon and defined to accentuate more fully the positive association that ought to exist between colleagues if they are to maximize their contributions to the improvement process. Consider, then, colleagues as helpers in the instructional improvement process, helpers in terms of five activities: observing instruction, mentoring, reviewing course materials, team teaching, and integrating and interpreting instructional information.

Observing Instruction. Faculty members need to be in each other's classrooms as helpers, not as evaluators. One way to encourage the helping role is to make the observations reciprocal, not something one does to the other but something that becomes a shared responsibility. The mutual vulnerability decreases the anxiety and helps ensure a real attempt at constructive communication after the observation. As already suggested in Chapter Four, faculty can be motivated and prepared if prior to a visit the two people involved view and discuss a videotaped teaching sample or visit the class of a third person with the purpose of sharing orientations to teaching in light of a specific example. The visit should also be grounded on the notion that the observer is just as likely to learn something important about his or her own teaching when visiting a colleague as when the colleague visits him or her.

Pairing faculty across departments reduces anxiety and helps to ensure that the focus is on teaching processes as opposed to content. Confidentiality is also easier to protect if the colleague is from across campus, not just down the hall. Moreover, not knowing the content encourages the colleague to view the instruction from that very important student perspective. "How would I be responding if I were required to take this class? When was I clear/confused about the content? When did I find my attention waning?"

Faculty are also encouraged to observe in each other's classes if those proposing the strategy offer a clear set of guidelines or outline a series of steps for the activity. This is a new experience for faculty, and because they may have old scars, a set of guidelines can go a long way to ensure a positive and constructive experience for the people involved.

Different steps or guidelines can be proposed; again, the

definitive collection has yet to be identified. The point is to offer *some* set and then suggest to faculty that they may adapt what is proposed to suit their needs, as long as they approach the activity systematically. To illustrate, consider the following outline for the activity. (See Resource B for a second illustration.) *First,* faculty meet for a preliminary discussion that fulfills three objectives. Initially, they share with each other their basic orientations to teaching, what they believe about the endeavor, how they know whether they have succeeded, why they keep trying, for example. The point here is to acquaint themselves with each other's pedagogical perspective. Next, they talk about the respective classes in which the observations will occur. They discuss their objectives for the course and for the day of the visit. They share any relevant material, including any assigned reading to be discussed that day. Finally, during the preliminary meeting, the instructors identify for each other the area(s) in which they would like to have feedback—what it is the colleague should specifically observe. Frequently, faculty have trouble here. They may not know the possible areas, or they may think that by virtue of identifying some, they are hiding others. Typically, faculty respond, "Oh make comments about whatever you like," essentially giving each other the same sort of license they give students when they ask what students liked most and least about a course. Instructors should be strongly counseled to identify the areas specifically. They need that protection, especially in the beginning, when they have no experience with colleagues as helpers. The colleague observer needs to know. She or he probably does not have much experience observing instruction and will do better given specific items to observe. In addition, this approach gives faculty the opportunity to receive feedback in areas of interest to them. A checklist can facilitate the process by identifying potential areas for feedback.

　　Second, colleagues visit each other's class. Focusing their attention on those aspects of the instruction they have identified, making notes during and after the observation, the colleagues aim for a descriptive account of what happened in each class. It is sometimes very effective for the instructor who is teaching also to make notes after the class, essentially completing an informal self-evaluation of the instruction. This way, when the colleagues meet, they *share* reactions, possibly using a checklist to guide the conversation. Self-evaluation works well to highlight different assessments. Both classes are visited before the conversation about the observations occurs. The conversation should not be scheduled immediately after the observations but should occur within a week of the visits.

Third, colleagues discuss the observations. The conversation, preferably held at a neutral site where the two will not be interrupted, should focus on the aspects of instruction identified as areas for feedback. The discussion should be descriptive. That is, when the colleague offers an opinion, for example, "I think you discourage kids from asking questions," he or she must support that opinion by identifying what the instructor did that prompted that conclusion. "When you ask if there are any questions, you only look at the class for a second; then you look down at your notes." "You only asked for student questions twice during the entire period." "One student in the back had her hand up for at least a minute before you stopped lecturing and recognized her." The instructor may argue that these behaviors do not communicate a lack of interest in student questions. Certainly the inference drawn from any behavior is up for debate. But the colleague emphasizes that those behaviors caused him or her to conclude that students were discouraged from asking questions. Colleagues should also be counseled to offer both negative and positive reactions. The conversation should always include an exploration of alternatives — what are some other ways of accomplishing the objectives, and which of those ways are best suited to the style of the instructor involved? Finally, the conversation needs to conclude with some discussion of next steps. Instructional observation is not an end in itself; it is a means to better teaching. What needs to happen next to ensure that that ultimate objective is obtained?

How might faculty be persuaded to try this kind of instructional observation? Sometimes testimonials encourage them to try new activities. If several well-respected faculty members can be encouraged to test the water, if it goes well, and if they will say so publicly, others can be persuaded. For example, the instructional development unit or department head interested in promoting the activity should convene a workshop, present the activity, provide any necessary background materials, offer to pair faculty with instructors from different departments, and help in any other appropriate way. If some faculty members decide to try it and then can be persuaded to share their experiences, a second session can be scheduled. If faculty participants shy away from public appearances, perhaps they could be persuaded to write a brief description of their experiences, which could then be circulated to members of the department, published in an in-house instructional development newsletter, or simply printed and attached to the set of guidelines distributed to interested faculty.

Getting faculty colleagues to observe each other once is only the first goal. They need to be in each other's classes regularly, routinely. To expect that to occur may be naive and unrealistic. Faculty labor under multiple demands. Nevertheless, observations such as these should not be a special, one-time activity. They need to be an ongoing part of teaching. They keep instructors fresh, encourage and develop accurate self-assessments, and make obvious the complexities of the teaching-learning phenomenon.

Alternative models and approaches to instructional observation can be used so that faculty do not tire of the activity, or because they better fit the culture of a particular institution, or because faculty themselves find them more appealing. Published information about several alternative approaches exists and can be used to devise a local version of the activity. For example Katz (1985) describes a strategy in which colleagues are paired and use an agenda that aims to discover more about the learning experiences of students enrolled in the class of the one being observed. The teacher and students in the class are given a learning style inventory and personality inventory. The observer interviews small groups of students and scrutinizes materials such as class notes and essay answers. Katz (1985, p. 6) writes of this approach to observation: "Making the student an object of study and engaging the student's collaboration in his or her own learning are prime conditions for the development of the art of teaching. Repeated interviews with the same students to learn how they have been responding to the materials and the teaching of a course have led both the students and their faculty interviewers to a heightened awareness of how students study and learn, and they have elicited valuable suggestions of how teachers might better reach their students."

Sweeney and Grasha (1979) propose organizing faculty into three-person groups in which all three function as observers and instructors. This plan has a particularly strong follow-up component in which each instructor targets an area for improvement. Skoog (1980, p. 23) describes a five-step observation cycle that is "specific in that the observee identifies problems and concerns to guide colleagues in observing, describing, and critiquing teaching."

As these various approaches illustrate, faculty have much to learn from each other about how they teach. Instructional observations enable them to learn firsthand. Predicating the visits on the idea of colleagues as helpers and having the participants review the instruction from the perspectives suggested reduce the anxiety these visits provoke and encourage constructive dialogue about the instruction observed and teaching in general. Instructional observation on these terms is an improvement strategy worth cultivating.

Mentoring. Academic traditions of collegiality do incorporate many of the "innovations" currently ascribed to mentoring. There has always been some expectation that old-timers will help newcomers learn the ropes in the department, that accepted definitions of scholarship will be shared, that the relative weights of teaching and research will be communicated informally. Faculty members were probably mentoring each other long before it was the trendy thing to do.

However, *instructional* mentoring is not as well established a practice in academic communities as it ought to be. Somehow classrooms are confused with castles and respect for privacy is so genuinely revered that not even the classrooms of new faculty members with no teaching experience are entered. Let the new faculty member get things under control, and then somebody will observe for the second-year review. Colleagues ought to do better for newcomers to the profession. Learning to teach while teaching for the first time is indeed a trial by fire that no one should pass through alone. There needs to be a confidant, guide, friend, a colleague helper who can offer seasoned advice and insights.

Of course, it is not always just the faculty member new to teaching who needs the insights. Students vary with institutions. Who they are, what they expect, and how they respond can all influence instructional style, as well as classroom policies and practices. One seasoned veteran the author knows recalls his unsettling experience at a new institution by sharing with all newcomers to the department the "five things I wish somebody had told me about students in this college when I first started teaching here."

The recent focus on mentoring has primarily drawn attention to the value of the activity for the "mentee"—the recipient of the wisdom and insights offered. In the academic realm and with an instructional improvement agenda in mind, the value of the mentoring to the person doing it should not be overlooked. Faculty who may not be particularly instructionally aware will find themselves considering instructional strategies, policies, and practices much more thoroughly if there is some expectation that they will serve as a mentor of new teachers. The attention and discussion have the potential to infuse what may be old and tired teaching with new ideas. Some empirical evidence describes the extent and degree to which that happens. Holmes (1988, p. 18) surveyed forty-four faculty mentors and asked them to identify any benefits they had received. Of the ten most frequently marked benefits, she writes, "Three of these . . . reflected increased contact with colleagues in other departments and colleges. The second most frequently reported benefit was increased enthusiasm for teaching. . . . Perhaps most surprising of all was the fact that 23 percent of the mentors said they had modified their teaching style as a direct result of serving as a mentor." The implications of these results for instructional improvers are important. If teaching can indeed be improved so unobtrusively, so cost-effectively, then mentoring activities ought to be given serious attention by those deciding which improvement strategies to propose to faculty.

Not all the recent attention focused on mentoring has been valuable. Mentoring programs of all sorts are "In," which means that many faculty may be benefiting from them, but the idea that mentoring must occur under the rubric of some programmatic structure prevents many faculty members and departments from considering the activity. Mentoring of all sorts, instructional mentoring in particular, can occur without some highly organized, expensive, labor-intensive, structured program. This is not to denigrate such programs; they work well, but the benefits they accrue can be gained by a more informal approach.

To illustrate, consider the following scenario. A college dean circulates a memo describing a mutually beneficial mentoring relationship between tenured faculty members and newcomers. Any faculty members interested in participating should so indicate. The dean sends a version of the memo to all new appointees — perhaps a bit more strongly urging their participation. At the beginning of the term, the mentors and mentees meet. They have been paired (across departments to ensure the instructional focus) either randomly or according to similarities in instructional responsibilities (those teaching labs paired with others teaching labs, and so on). At the informal gathering, the pairs are given a list of possible activities that might profitably engage them during the semester. The list could include many of the activities mentioned in earlier chapters: a reading program, classes they might both observe, diagnostic student evaluation activities in which to participate jointly, seminars and programs they might jointly attend, or several open discussions scheduled for all faculty participating in the activity. (For a sample list, see Weimer, 1989). The list should also propose less structured activities, for example, simply meeting on a regular basis to talk about whatever instructional issues are of concern or present themselves. Each pair might meet once a month for lunch or to take a walk together. Those proposing the activities make no prescriptions as to the number of meetings or how many

activities ought to be completed and require no formal reporting procedures. At the end of the semester, the group reconvenes
to share experiences and reactions.

A loosely organized and uncontrolled structure such as
this probably does not qualify as a "mentoring program" in any
official sense. Nonetheless, this approach does utilize the premises of effective improvement strategies discussed elsewhere in
this volume. Granted, some pairs probably will not get organized
and accomplish much of substance. But mentoring, like instructional improvement generally, is much less effective when it ends
up being something done by one person to another. Moreover,
the model proposed shifts the responsibility for action onto the
pairs, especially on the senior faculty member assuming the role
of mentor. It ends up being an unobtrusive but effective way
of motivating faculty members to make changes in their teaching — to say nothing of the benefits to the less experienced instructor.

Mentoring, especially if the attention can be focused on
the teaching, offers many attractive possibilities for instructional
improvers. Once again, though, the very tenets of mentoring
are violated if ever the mentor moves from the position of confidant, guide, and helper to that of judge.

Reviewing Course Materials. Colleagues are in an excellent
position to help each other with course materials. Once again,
despite this obvious role and function for colleagues, few do share
course materials with each other, especially when objectives are
exclusively formative. This means that those proposing the
strategy must be explicit in identifying activities that might occur under the course materials review rubric and in describing
their benefits.

For starters, students often suffer from the poor test construction skills of faculty. Yet students are in an impossible position when it comes to arguing about exams. Their interest is
simply too vested. As a result, faculty many times do not listen
to students when they should. A colleague can be most helpful
in responding to student objections. One faculty member once
told the author that for years students had complained that his

tests were too long—they never had enough time to complete them during the period. He reported that he could do the problems in half an hour. He knew he would be faster than students, but they had an hour. He believed he was getting a bum rap. Once when recounting his woes to a colleague, the colleague (who knew the content but did not teach it) volunteered to spend an evening reviewing the material to be covered on the next exam and then to take the exam in the prescribed time period. When the time was up, the colleague still had three problems to do. As the faculty member reports, "That's how I learned my tests were in fact too long." In the same vein, it is common knowledge that multiple-choice items often contain inadvertent clues about the correct answer. If a colleague not taking the class, not doing the reading, and not particularly familiar with the content can get a B on the exam, that fact should encourage the test maker to look closely at the items.

The converse applies as well. A near knock-down-drag-out argument occurred between two physicists who (after many, many complaints from students) agreed to take each other's exams. They both got C's. They argued passionately about the items on the tests, the wording of the problems, and the assigning of partial credit. The discussion was probably more heated than it should have been, but what a valuable lesson in the potential of tests themselves to compromise what those who take them may know very well.

Colleagues need not focus exclusively on exams. They can profitably look at syllabi from courses and offer reactions on the design and weight of assignments. Are the reading assignments too lengthy? Ask a colleague to read a set of unfamiliar material and report how long it took. Yes, the colleague will read more quickly and insightfully than students, but if it took the colleague an hour and a half to wade through half the reading, then when students announce that it takes them three hours to do the reading, they may be telling the truth.

Colleague input of this kind should be descriptive. The colleague does not speak for all the students in the class. The colleague reports how the material impressed her or him. The colleague may make recommendations, but those are not mandates for change; they are simply the informed (and one would hope respected) opinions of one who shares a vested interest in creating course materials that cultivate student learning.

Team Teaching. In the late sixties and early seventies, team teaching took colleges and universities by storm. Since then, interest in the activity has waned and all but died. Some faculty today still do what they call team teaching, but it is a far cry from the truly shared instructional responsibilities that characterized early versions of the activity. Then faculty did design and plan the course together, did go to class together, and often even shared the same podium, exchanging ideas and sometimes arguments in front of students. Today when faculty members "team teach," they divide course responsibilities in half (or thirds or even fourths), each doing his or her own portion, sharing only the course number.

The current version of team teaching holds little potential to improve instruction. On the other hand, when faculty truly share the responsibility for a course, few report participating in the experience without its having significant effects on their instruction. The experience can be especially significant for faculty new to college teaching if the other member of the team adopts the colleague-as-helper role.

Integrating and Interpreting Instructional Information. The colleague role of integrating and interpreting instructional information was first proposed by Cohen and McKeachie (1980, p. 153): "Perhaps the greatest evaluative role faculty may serve is to integrate information on teaching effectiveness. Colleagues are in a unique position to view information from sources such as student, peer, and self-ratings within the context of certain course-setting characteristics." Colleagues do have the objectivity necessary to look at student evaluation results from different courses across a number of semesters. They are also in a good position to connect the specific details of a formative assessment with the global results of summative evaluations. They can help faculty make the translation from abstract descriptions of teaching to the concrete behaviors of instruction, especially when they visit the classroom. As Cohen and McKeachie conclude, "The potential of this role needs to be explored further."

Summary

Colleagues can and should play a fundamental role in instructional improvement. In this effort, they can continue unique and valuable assistance as reviewers and helpers. Menges (1987, p. 91) offers a concluding qualification and further evidence of the value of colleagues in instructional improvement: "Effectiveness of colleagues as consultants in the teaching improvement process has yet to be validated against criteria of student learning. As far as faculty participants are concerned, however, findings are clear: participants report high satisfaction, more interaction with other faculty members, increased motivation, and renewed interest in teaching."

7

◆◆◆◆◆◆◆◆◆◆◆◆◆◆◆◆◆◆◆◆◆◆◆◆◆◆◆◆◆◆◆

Supportive
Academic Leaders

THE CLIMATE for teaching and learning at too many institutions
is not conducive to maintaining or improving instructional health
and well-being. Even at institutions with teaching missions and
public commitments to instructional excellence, the climate could
be improved. In response, this chapter aims to describe the situation not as it is but as it should be. What sort of institutional
climate encourages, supports, and otherwise makes possible instructional excellence? What sort of environment is needed if
the activities described in Chapters Four, Five, and Six are, in
fact, to improve college teaching? Describing the climate is the
first step in answering these questions, but descriptions do not
improve instruction. A constructive teaching-learning climate
must be created, and this chapter proposes a key role for academic leaders (including department heads, deans, academic
vice presidents, and provosts) in the process. The overarching
intent, then, is to put the improvement process and activities
proposed into some context, some environment, some departmental or institutional setting where their potential benefits can
be realized to the fullest extent.

A Climate for Instructional Improvement

It may help to begin by establishing the meaning of the
words *climate* and *environment* because in the present context they
have nothing to do with the weather or the effects of surrounding ecological conditions. Rather, in the sense used here, these
terms indicate the collection of social and cultural conditions

130

in which one lives and works and that influences, in some cases determines, the quality of life. All that surrounds the process of education as it occurs in our colleges and universities affects behavior within the academic community.

Certain of those conditions affect what faculty members believe and do about instructional improvement. Chapter One has identified several factors that discourage or even prevent faculty from making a commitment to better teaching. There is no need to reiterate them here; rather, the goal now is to describe an alternative teaching-learning climate that can effectively dissuade faculty from the attitudes and assumptions that currently impede the instructional improvement process. The climate metaphor clarifies the point. If the climate is hot, wool clothing is discarded and replaced with light-weight fabrics. If the teaching-learning climate is fair, then heavy, negative, and cynical assumptions about its improvement are much more readily removed.

One can discover something about the favorable conditions for instructional improvement by considering what is known about climates conducive to student learning. After all, the instructional improvement agenda at its heart proposes that faculty "learn" more about teaching. Moore (1976) identifies several dimensions of climates for learning that seem relevant or adaptable to this context. He suggests that students learn well in climates of *inquiry* — environments in which the questions outnumber the answers, in which the focus is as much on asking questions as it is on answering them. That same spirit of inquiry needs to be applied to teaching; there needs to be some recognition of teaching as a phenomenon in its own right (not some skill subsumed in knowledge of content) and some generally accepted sense that we still have much to learn about the process of "educating" students. Faculty most fundamentally, but also the academic community at large, should have the sense of being joined together in the quest to discover more about effective teaching and learning. Questions about teaching should be encouraged, valued, and deliberated. The spirit of inquiry already characterizes much about the university environment. It drives the research enterprise. Extending that sense of questioning to instructional issues seems natural. Perhaps part of the answer here involves a redefinition of scholarship so that the study and inquiry that are necessarily a part of effective instruction are included and do count favorably in the promotion and tenure process.

Moore also writes about climates of *clarity,* environments in which expectations are understood. The student understands what it is she or he needs to do. Yet university environments frequently do confuse the signals. Faculty hear that teaching is important but see that research is rewarded. The point here is not a restatement of the old argument that teaching needs to be rewarded but that university leaders need to be clear and consistent in communicating expectations to faculty. The extent to which both teaching and research are valued needs to be explicitly stated. Faculty are frustrated and confused when teaching is valued enough to say so but not to do so. That frustrates them far more than the fact that research universities, by their very nature and purpose, are never going to be as committed to instructional excellence as institutions with more explicit teaching missions. Prerequisite to all this is the need for colleges and universities to know who they are and what they can accomplish. There is no need for every college in the country to look to the future with an eye toward becoming a major research university. The objective is unrealistic and unnecessary. There is a very real need for institutions to understand, accept, and act upon their own identities, missions, and goals. Bland and Schmitz (1988, p. 203) found this recommendation over and over in their review of literature and research on faculty vitality. Of the 152 specific recommendations reviewed, they write, "The most frequent kind of recommendation we encountered stressed the essential, critical link between faculty development and institutional mission and policies, a link that can only be achieved if each party acknowledges its role."

Students also learn better in climates of *confidence,* according to Moore. The idea here is to create in the classroom an atmosphere in which students are given many opportunities to succeed, where their progress is measured regularly, in small steps, and they are motivated to keep trying by the visible belief of the teacher in their commitment and ability to succeed. What an excellent set of conditions under which to pursue the improvement of instruction. Instructors, too, need to feel that they are being given opportunities to succeed. Learning to teach well is not an easy task to be accomplished painlessly during a bit of release time. It requires an ongoing commitment and the chance to succeed (and fail) at steps along the way. Students (and instructors, as well) are motivated to keep trying when their efforts, their determination, and their willingness to try again are recognized. They need encouragement, from each other and from the person in charge.

Classrooms need to be places of *instructional alternatives*. In this context, Moore writes about the need to use a variety of teaching methods. This climate recognizes the inherent diversity of students and encourages college teachers to mold learning tasks to students' needs and proclivities. Recognition of instructional diversity also contributes to the improvement of teaching. There is no one correct way to teach. Faculty need to explore methods and strategies that fit the configurations of the content they must teach, the instructional setting in which the teaching occurs, and the individual dimensions of their own teaching style.

Respect for diversity has another dimension as well. Many faculty members today berate students for no longer being willing to take risks. Many students would rather avoid making choices; they like having instructors tell them exactly what they need to do: "What do you want in this paper?" As in many other instances, this student response reflects a corresponding dimension of the way many faculty teach. How often do instructors take risks in class? Too many of them, consistently, course after course, year after year, use the standard, tried, and true teaching techniques. Where is the spirit of adventure, exploration, discovery, and conquest that ought to characterize efforts to teach well? They only rarely appear. Why? Because the conditions for teaching in most institutions do not prescribe or cultivate them. Most faculty prefer to play it safe, especially when signals about expectations are unclear. College teachers would be more inclined to take risks if they taught in an environment that recognized, valued, and cultivated instructional diversity.

Finally, not identified by Moore but so obvious that it almost bears no repeating, faculty will teach better in climates that recognize and reward instructional excellence. How many hundreds of times has this been pointed out? Why is such an obvious condition to good teaching ignored so consistently? Are faculty impossible to please? Or is good teaching impossible to recognize and reward?

Part of the answer to all those questions relates to the already discussed contradiction between word and deed in regard to the importance of teaching. At virtually every institution in the business of higher education, some well-intentioned administrator, frequently the chief administrator, has asserted the importance of teaching, said that it matters at the institution. That is not enough. In fact, such statements actually contribute negatively to the environment for teaching and its improvement when administrative actions contradict the statements. Saying does not make it so; doing does.

This naturally leads to the issue of reward and recognition. The most obvious and easiest solution is to make teaching count at promotion and tenure time. For reasons not relevant to the discussion at hand, many institutions do not do this. Some of those institutions have tried to create an atmosphere of reward by establishing teaching awards. In theory the idea sounds good; in practice it does not always work. Arrowsmith (1967, pp. 57–58) uses a metaphor to explain why: "At present, the universities are as uncongenial to teaching as the Mojave Desert is to a clutch of Druid priests. If you want to restore a Druid priesthood, you cannot do it by offering prizes for Druid-of-the-Year. If you want Druids, you must grow forests."

In other words, the problem with many teaching awards from the faculty perspective is that they smack of tokenism — "a partial or minimal fulfillment of obligations, as in a token effort." They acknowledge only superior teaching skills and leave the thorny issue of tenured, inferior skills untouched. Most important, such awards often leave faculty recipients unconvinced that the value of their contributions have been truly recognized. One faculty recipient (Middleton, 1987, p. 3) writes poignantly of an experience typical for many instructors.

First, I can say that it brought immense personal satisfaction. The award assured me that despite my sporadic feelings of despondency about the value of what I was doing, at least some of my colleagues and students thought my efforts were worthwhile. That has given me a boost and confidence in the feeling that, yes, the effort to be an effective teacher was worthwhile.

Second, it has brought a tinge of sadness because the nomination procedure seemed so haphazard. I know of colleagues who have not been recognized and who are more worthy of recognition than I am. Alternatively, I know of individuals who have actively campaigned for the award, whose credibility is suspect, and yet who have been honored. This has led to a "devaluation of the currency" in the eyes of some. As a result, whether through jealousy or genuine knowledge, colleagues have suggested the winning of the award is of no great significance.

Third, I doubt if the award has even been noticed by the university. Oh yes, I have received the polite letter from the president's office and comments from colleagues whom I respect, but I feel it has had no impact upon my career. I am not bitter about that because of the personal satisfaction gained. However, where it "counts" at the time of promotion, tenure and merit considerations, the award made no difference to my merit ratings and I remained at the same rank at which I was at the time of the award.

Fourth, the award is viewed very much as a *teaching* honor. As such it is immediately second-rate. Had I been made a fellow of my professional society, *that* would have been a noteworthy achievement. However, at least at this university, the attitude prevails that teaching occurs in a 50-minute lecture or lab and as such cannot really be viewed as a serious, scholarly endeavor. Thus for me, teaching awards still fall into the category of tokenism.

This aspect of tokenism is not an inherent part of teaching awards. It results rather from the way in which they are used, the policies, practices, and procedures that surround them. They can positively contribute to an institution's teaching environment. They do not do so when they represent the institution's only commitment to instructional excellence. If a university has 3,000 faculty members and bestows three teaching awards per year, the sense of tokenism and the awards' inability to motivate faculty to better teaching are obvious. Teaching awards work successfully when they represent one of many ways in which instructional excellence and efforts to achieve it are recognized, valued, and rewarded.

To summarize, then, the instructional climate does influence the quality of teaching that occurs within it. Some climates influence that quality more constructively than others. Institutions that want to cultivate instructional excellence should commit themselves to creating a climate where vigorous intellectual exchanges occur over instructional matters, where the words and deeds of those in power communicate clear and consistent messages about the value of good teaching, where the need for continued and concerted attention to teaching is recognized and supported, where instructional diversity and innovation are encouraged and valued, and where all personnel decisions reflect the institution's commitment to instructional quality, be that quality superior or inferior.

Creating the Climate

As important as describing the climate is advice on creating it. The potential of an institution's academic leaders in making this happen exceeds that of an individual faculty member. Certainly individual faculty members can model instructional attitudes and activities that will influence the classroom decisions of their colleagues, but department heads, college administrators, and central administrators are in positions that enable them to influence larger numbers of faculty members much more directly. This is not to discourage individuals who wish to contribute to a more positive instructional environment at their institutions — only to make them realistic about what they can accomplish *and* to encourage academic leaders to take a more active role in creating and contributing to a constructive teaching and learning climate. The Bland and Schmitz (1988, p. 205) review leads the authors to a more emphatic conclusion: "The recommendations point out that administrators *should* be and *have* to be involved in order for renewal to be successful."

As far as creating the climate, academic leaders do that by adopting policies and advocating and participating in activities that demonstrate components of a healthy instructional environment. They can do this explicitly in terms of each of the individual dimensions of the climate just discussed.

To promote a climate of *inquiry* about teaching, academic leaders should routinely and regularly raise instructional issues — in department meetings, in committee meetings, in private, in informal interactions, and in other appropriate gatherings. The objective should be to focus on the nature of the teaching-learning enterprise in general, not on the teaching of the individual. Are we doing enough in this department to eliminate student passivity? How do we design exam experiences that promote learning? Are we teaching too much content and not enough process?

Department heads can and should regularly circulate materials on teaching and learning to faculty members. Always the tone is constructive. Materials are not distributed because faculty in the department need them. They are distributed because they are informative, interesting, and because we need to keep our instructional goals always before us.

Academic leaders help to create a climate of *clarity* when they make explicit the expectations of the department and the institution. New faculty get written materials documenting those expectations. Those materials are delivered personally in the context of a private meeting with each new appointee. Academic leaders make themselves accessible to new faculty — able, willing, and ready to answer questions about expectations.

Academic leaders should adopt the principle of saying less and doing more about the importance of teaching. Actions do speak more eloquently than words, especially when it comes to the reward and recognition of teaching. All sorts of actions convey the importance of teaching. Faculty can be encouraged to explore "scholarly" issues that derive from teaching experiences.

Publications about teaching need to count at promotion and tenure time. Departmental travel funds should be available to faculty interested in attending national meetings on teaching and learning. A number of excellent meetings occur regularly. Some solicit paper and program proposals on instructional issues; others offer opportunities to learn more about college teaching.

At the college or division level, some administrators at larger universities appoint ad hoc committees charged with looking after the instructional environment at an institution. Such committees concern themselves with a wide variety of issues all the way from the physical realities of the classroom (Is it clean? Well lighted? Comfortable? In need of renovation?) to generating guidelines governing appropriate instructional experiences for new TAs and/or professors new to college teaching. These committees are particularly good at raising levels of awareness and keeping instructional issues before the university community. To be effective, however, they must be empowered committees. They need to be able to influence policy and practice. They need to be able to do something about the instructional environment at the institution. Administrative actions such as these and many others do contribute to a climate of clarity, a climate in which academic leaders do something besides say that teaching is important.

Academic leaders can also be instrumental in creating a climate of *confidence*. As already discussed, an excessively evaluative environment inhibits the needed exchange of ideas and information about teaching. Those in charge need to de-emphasize the assessment aspects of instruction. This does not mean that they should be done away with. Faculty should be accountable for the instruction they provide, but the focus is not on that assessment but on activities that make the assessment outcome a foregone conclusion. These activities are seen as requiring work, commitment, and perseverance.

Academic leaders, just like the rest of the faculty, must understand that good teachers are made and not made easily. The pursuit of instructional excellence is a shared endeavor, not just an activity targeted for those who need it. Academic leaders should expect all instructors to continue their development as teachers. In the case of a department's experienced and effective instructors, the expectation may be that those faculty contribute to the development of the department's new and less experienced teachers.

Finally, academic leaders, including those at the department level and those in more central administrative positions, should not send faculty on the quest for good teaching unaided. Specifically, this means that if an institution expects faculty members to improve, it must make available resources and services to support that development. These may take the form of some instructional/faculty development center (a number of models are reviewed in the next chapters) or a more decentralized collection of resources and services. Not all the models require large budget allocations. Many of the most effective services will be those that do nothing more than coordinate faculty activities. To whatever degree possible, in whatever form best suits the institution, the principle must be recognized: If improvement is expected, its pursuit must be supported.

As for creating opportunities for *instructional alternatives* or diversity, again academic leaders are in positions to make significant contributions. The notion is that teaching will improve in a climate where faculty are encouraged to explore teaching methods and strategies that fit the configuration of the content, the instructional setting, and the proclivities of their teaching style. Part of creating this environment involves being able to propose alternatives to faculty, alternatives such as team teaching in which faculty truly do share responsibilities in a single course (not just divide the content and each teach a part), or experimental or theme courses that cross disciplinary boundaries, or courses that incorporate computer components. Faculty with new instructional ideas need to be encouraged. Instructional innovation grant programs such as those described in Chapter Five help implement these new ideas. Certainly alternative courses and teaching assignments challenge the bureaucratic structure that governs university operations. Expediting them requires work, but when faculty see administrators expending the effort, they see another tangible proof that teaching matters, that the institution is willing to support their interests and efforts.

This aspect of creating an environment conducive to instructional improvement is especially important in keeping the teaching of an individual faculty member fresh and invigorated across a number of years. As already discussed, teaching ruts are easy to fall into, especially when the teaching assignment stays the same year after year. Academic leaders, especially at the department level, can do much to keep faculty out of ruts. Teaching assignments need to change, not every semester or every course but more than once every five years. Changes go down more easily if people have plenty of lead time. If the course is a new one for a faculty member, out of his or her area of expertise, the opportunity to sit in the same course taught by a colleague ought to be available and/or some release time should be provided to facilitate the preparation. If teaching assignments are too difficult to change, then the curriculum may need to be modified: new courses offered, old ones combined, some old ones even deleted. Changing teaching assignments and courses is not always easy, especially if the tradition of change has not been established. The key is to establish the principle gradually. Despite the difficulties, instructional quality can only be helped in a climate where teachers and courses do not stagnate.

Change is only one part of creating a climate of diversity, however. The diversity also implies a recognition that not all faculty have the same requirements for instructional success. Some do better if they teach in the morning; others do not come to life until noon. Some can handle large classes; others wither and die in front of large crowds. Some thrive on teaching freshmen the basics; others need mature students, at least once in a while. Merit or worth should not be ascribed to differences like these. The contribution of the faculty member who teaches the introductory course should be valued just as much as the contribution of the faculty member who teaches the department's capstone course for majors.

In most departments, however, faculty skills and faculty preferences do not divide themselves evenly across the curriculum. In many departments (probably because all teaching assignments are not valued equally) too many faculty aspire to teach the capstone course and too few the introductory course. Or too many function best between 10 A.M. and noon on Tuesday, Wednesday, and Thursday and too few at 8 A.M. or 4:30 P.M. on Monday and Friday. In either event, the department head or whoever makes teaching assignments needs to be able to distinguish between skills and preferences. Many faculty (like many other people) "prefer" to sleep late; they can and do function fine at 8 A.M. if they are required to do so, and most will not object as long as they are not always called upon to teach the 8 A.M. class. In other words, everyone in the department shares the less desirable duties. However, the person making decisions about who teaches what and when balances preferences, needs, and skills so that faculty have as many opportunities as possible to teach under the conditions they deem most desirable while at the same time preventing them from sliding into comfortable ruts.

To complicate the decision making still further, recognition of diversity also implies the acknowledgment that instructional needs do not stay the same throughout a career. A new faculty member with little teaching experience does not need to acquire that experience with 200 lower-division students in the department's service course. That is not one of the hurdles new faculty should be expected to jump through on their way to becoming bonafide members of the department. Team teaching experiences can be especially helpful to new faculty members provided they occur in a climate of openness and trust where their exploration of teaching style is encouraged and supported.

Finally, teaching will improve in a climate where instructional excellence is recognized and rewarded. How do academic leaders accomplish that? First, they do what they can to make teaching count at promotion and tenure time. That is the bottom line and has been written about so many times that to belabor it is useless.

In addition, some creative alternatives to the typical teaching awards are beginning to emerge. Miami-Dade Community College (McCabe, 1986) in Florida is in the midst of establishing endowed teaching chairs much like research chairs currently a part of many universities. Faculty members occupy these chairs for a defined period (say, three years) during which they receive a healthy salary supplement and institutional support to pursue instructional issues of interest. The 3M Company in Canada (Weimer, 1987e) recently initiated a program that recognizes outstanding university teachers across Canada. The interesting dimension of this award is that it brings recipients together and charges them to further instructional excellence at their own universities as well as those throughout the country by serving as spokespersons and advocates for good teaching. Those wishing to cultivate a climate conducive to instructional excellence should explore the use of these models and new ones. The point made earlier bears repeating. Teaching awards can contribute a great deal to the instructional excellence of an institution only when they are one of several means used to value instruction. They must be part of a larger scheme of assessing teaching throughout the institution.

After one clearly understands what constitutes a climate for instructional excellence, ways to create that climate become obvious. As illustrated in this discussion, both large and small actions create and sustain the environment. Some will cost an institution money; others will cost in terms of time and commitment. All are worth the investment if an institution aspires to instructional quality. No prescribed set of activities is "right" or "enough" to create the desired climate. What works best will be tied to the culture of the institution and the individuals who lead it. The intent here is to provide a launching pad from which individually suited paths can be plotted.

Leadership

The issue of leadership is much discussed by academics and everyone else. The consensus seems to be that leadership is not what it once was or what it should be. Bennis and Nanus (1985, p. 2) write of the need for leadership in a book that uses interviews with ninety very different leaders to propose an alternative theory of leadership. "The need was never so great. A chronic crisis of governance — that is, the pervasive incapacity of organizations to cope with the expectations of their constituents — is now an overwhelming factor worldwide. If there was ever a moment in history when a comprehensive strategic view of leadership was needed, not just by a few leaders in high office but by large numbers of leaders in every job . . . this is certainly it." Although not all would agree, some would contend that this same crisis of leadership threatens our colleges and universities as well. The intent here is not to establish the existence of that crisis but only to assert that some believe that it exists. Even the possibility of its presence should be enough to encourage those in administrative posts at colleges and universities to be mindful of their positions as leaders.

Faculty, like other people, look to their leaders for all sorts of abstract qualities and characteristics. They look for role models. Sometimes this makes leaders nervous. It makes faculty nervous when students respond to them as people that they decide they do or do not want to be like. Nervous or not, having one's personhood scrutinized comes with the territory when one occupies a position at the front of the group.

Given this fact, academic leaders must not underestimate the power of their own example to motivate faculty to pursue instructional excellence. Most department heads and many administrators are faculty members themselves; a fair number still teach. Those who do not should, at least on occasion. Teaching provides an opportunity to model all the behaviors expected of faculty committed to effective instruction. This does not mean that the department head or dean must be the best teacher in the department. It does mean that the department head should be using diagnostic feedback tools, should be acquiring input from students and colleagues as to the impact of the teaching policies and practices he or she is using, should be talking about teaching with others, and should be updating, revising, and otherwise changing the course to keep it fresh.

A small but important distinction needs to be made here or the department head wishing to encourage faculty involvement in improvement will end up much like the teacher who thinks effective teaching is only a matter of regularly using five or six surefire strategies. Neither good teaching nor effective leadership is that simple. The quest for good teaching cannot be faked. Whether department head, dean, or faculty member, the leader will not convince by the strategies themselves or the example he or she offers by using them unless they are accompanied by honest commitment and serious intent.

Too often "leadership" gets lost in the push to handle more paper, manage one's time, juggle limited funds, and strategically plan for coming years, activities that improve instruction only incidentally. The other activities identified in this chapter respond to faculty leadership needs much more directly and effectively.

Conclusion

Several years ago, the Group for Human Development in Higher Education (1974, p. 20) described the task confronting academic leaders who wished to create a teaching-learning climate conducive to improvement: "Building a system of support for teaching is no less complex than creating an audience for the arts while supporting their practice and training young performers and artists." More than fifteen years later, the task remains, in essence, still to be tackled. Perhaps the reaffirmation of its importance and advice on ways to proceed will encourage some academic leaders to accept the challenge.

◆◆◆◆◆◆◆◆◆◆◆◆◆◆◆◆◆◆◆◆◆◆◆◆◆◆◆◆◆◆◆◆◆

PART THREE

INSTITUTIONAL OPTIONS FOR IMPROVING COLLEGE TEACHING

8

✦✦✦✦✦✦✦✦✦✦✦✦✦✦✦✦✦✦✦✦✦✦✦✦✦✦✦✦✦

Organizational
and Administrative
Approaches

ONE OPTION for academic leaders and others serious about creating a climate conducive to instructional health and well-being
is to centralize the resources and services discussed in Chapter
Seven by assigning an administrator the responsibility for them
or creating a teaching center or some form of instructional development program. The consideration of a programmatic response
to instructional needs raises a bevy of questions: How is this
kind of unit organized? To whom should people assigned instructional development duties report? Where should such a unit
be located in an institution's organizational structure? What
training and background are necessary for people assigned
responsibilities in this area? What is needed in the way of personnel to run an instructional improvement program? How
much does it cost to begin and sustain one? How should the
unit's resources and services be evaluated? What if an institution cannot afford this kind of full-scale programmatic response?
Are there viable alternatives?

   Instructional and faculty development programs, as well
as other centralized services in support of teaching, have been
around in various forms for more than twenty years. If we begin
with a brief history that creates a sense of perspective, we can
answer all these questions. We know how programs have been
and are currently organized. We know where they are tied into
the university structure, who runs them, what kind of staffs they
have, and how much institutions spend to support their activities.

Viable alternatives do exist and have functioned successfully at a number of different institutions.

There is a problem with the answers to these organizational and operational questions, however. For every question, there is more than one answer, and choosing the "right" one depends on a host of variables that tend to be institutionally specific. In other words, what works at one place is not guaranteed to work at another place. For this reason, this chapter must do more than present the organizational and operational details. It must offer some guidelines that can direct institutions to the "right" choices. It does this by explaining why and how an institution's specific culture needs to guide decision making and by showing the decision making in action via a hypothetical example.

Instructional and Faculty Development: A Brief History

Before we review the various organizational details associated with the programmatic improvement of instruction, it is important to see the current wave of interest in the area in light of its historical context. This is not the first time that institutions have considered the role of instructional development programs, units, centers, and/or directors. A good review of the early history is offered by Mathis (1979).

The present is an interesting time in the faculty/instructional development movement. With its nearly twenty-year history, the movement has come of age, and not all the growing up has been easy. In the beginning, the movement led a charmed existence. A number of foundations (Bush and Murdock, for example), made large open-ended grants to institutions to pursue what was then more commonly called faculty development. And institutions did pursue it, leaving behind administrative structures and lots of fine activities and program ideas. Unfortunately, in spite of this auspicious beginning, when soft monies ran out and universities first confronted the realities of retrenchment, faculty development all but died. Many major programs around the country were cut; others hunkered down and became very realistic about what they could and could not do for faculty if they were to survive. A number of programs weathered the storm and are now being joined by newcomers. Perhaps because of the national attention presently being directed toward college teaching, interest in faculty/instructional development is once again genuine and widespread.

A brief look at the history of these programmatic efforts also gives some clues as to their numbers and the length of their life spans. Centra (1978) completed the first nationwide survey to establish how many institutions had organized programs or sets of practices aimed at improving instruction. In 1975 he sent a letter to the presidents of all 2,600 degree-granting institutions in the country. Approximately 60 percent of the 1,783 respondents indicated that they did have organized programs and practices designed to improve instruction. A follow-up survey was mailed to program/activity coordinators, and from their responses Centra (1978) determined that 44 percent of them were at institutions with programs. Erickson (1986) modified and repeated the original survey and reported that 44 percent of the 630 schools responding to his survey claimed such a person or unit. An encouraging 66 percent of those surveyed by Erickson indicated that "their institutions' current investment in faculty, instructional, and professional development was much or somewhat greater than it had been only three years earlier" (p. 183).

Despite this evidence of expansion, many instructional development programs appear to have short life spans. Among the Erickson (1986) survey respondents, a full 50 percent indicated that the current program had been created since 1981. In the Centra (1978) survey, the mean length of existence for the units was 2.3 years. Gustafson and Bratton (1984, p. 2) randomly selected and surveyed 72 instructional improvement centers from a list of 275 published by Gaff (1975) "to determine their current status." Seventy-two of these centers were still in operation.

Major Organizational Options

It is important to note that the surveys mentioned above and most other published materials consider instructional improvement and faculty development jointly. In other words, not all the sources share the exclusively pedagogical orientation of this book. The commingling of other faculty and professional development areas with instructional improvement activities is considered in this section. What resources, services, and responsibilities are combined in any given organizational structure has a significant effect on the operation and outcomes of the program.

Organizational and operational matters are considered in the context of three major organizational options: (1) those in which the instructional improvement impetus is given to an *individual,* typically an administrator or consultant; (2) those in which the resources and services are sponsored by a *committee,* generally composed of *faculty members;* and (3) those in which the activities emanate from a *program, office, unit,* or *center* structure. In the balance of this section, the various options available within each structure are reviewed, along with relevant operational details, and each approach is assessed in terms of its major strengths and weaknesses.

The Administrator/Consultant Option. Instructional development responsibilities can be assigned to an individual. In a few cases this person is a consultant. However, according to Erickson (1986), most often the individual is an administrator who assumes instructional development duties as one of a collection of other responsibilities. Erickson's survey further reveals that the most common structural approach to instructional development is the arrangement whereby a faculty committee works with or advises the appointed administrator.

The chief advantage of this approach is cost. With an administrator and an advisory faculty committee guiding the instructional development, all available money can be directed to program activities. However, the administrator and faculty have many other duties, little time, and probably not a lot of motivation to delve into the complexities of instructional development strategies and techniques. As a result, most of what happens at institutions with this kind of instructional improvement arrangement involves workshop/seminar activities. The administrator has the budget to pay for and the clerical support to arrange the details. An outside expert comes to campus for a day and conducts a seminar or a retreat that faculty are all but required to attend, the appropriate faculty committee evaluates the program, and instructional development obligations are fulfilled for that semester.

The Erickson (1986) survey documents the fact that this approach severely limits both the kind and quantity of services that can be made available to faculty. "Fewest services were available on campuses where faculty development was one among many of an administrator's responsibilities" (p. 185). However, the recurring refrain of this book is that something is better than nothing. If this approach meets current budget constraints, assigning instructional development responsibilities to an administrator is better than no institutional recognition of the need to support faculty efforts in the classroom. Administrators with limited time and resources should consider the variety of alternative activities proposed in Chapters Five and Six. Some of the economical and efficient possibilities have more enduring effects than the once-a-semester workshop exhibition.

There is at least one other disadvantage to the individual administrator model. Assigning an administrator responsibility to help faculty "improve" potentially inhibits the process — for many of the same reasons that were discussed in the context of evaluating and improving instruction. The administrator, if not directly, certainly by virtue of association, belongs to the group that ultimately renders personnel decisions. This makes it especially difficult for faculty in trouble to divulge the nature of their instructional problems. In general, then, the instruction that most needs to be improved gets no direct attention in this approach. On the other hand, bogus interest in improvement occurs as a result of certain faculty members' need to impress certain administrators of their sincerity.

Nevertheless, some versions of the individual option do circumvent its limitations. One of the most promising of these is described by Bakker and Lacey (1980), who recount experiences with a "teaching consultant" at Earlham College. This senior faculty member is chosen by faculty committees to listen to and interact with fellow faculty members as a sympathetic colleague. Bakker and Lacey describe further: "The Consultant is *not* a developer, if by that term is meant someone who comes along and improves a piece of waste or undeveloped real estate by putting his or her own impress on it. Ideally, the Consultant should have no agenda except to reflect with the Consultee about teaching, to take the Consultee's perception of need and description of teaching goals as the starting-point for any work" (p. 35).

In this model, the faculty member functions in the consultant capacity on a half-time basis. The rest of the time is spent teaching. The consultant serves a fixed term appointment in the position (either two or three years) and respects the confidentiality of faculty. In fact, the consultant is not allowed to serve on any promotion and tenure committee during the period of the appointment.

In terms of advantages, this approach accrues a similar economic benefit. Because the consultant works with individual faculty members, discussing and observing instruction firsthand as it occurs, the effects of these interventions tend to be more enduring than those resulting from infrequent workshop participation. Being a faculty member at the institution makes it likely that the consultant understands the institution and the kinds of students it enrolls. The advice offered therefore tends to have more credibility. Moreover, respect for confidentiality makes it safe for faculty members to divulge details of instructional difficulties.

The approach is not without limitations, however. With how many college teachers can one faculty member, doing the job half-time, consult? What does even a senior faculty member know (other than experientially) about good teaching and, more importantly, about how faculty members implement instructional alternations that make a difference in their teaching effectiveness? Nonetheless, the potential of this approach to change instructional practices must be weighed against these limitations. Bakker and Lacey (1980) are very optimistic about it, especially when it is used at institutions committed to instructional excellence, when the college is relatively small and church related. Bakker and Lacey also believe that the approach can be modified to fit a variety of institutional needs and ways of operating.

One final type of individual option deserves consideration: the consortium model. In this case, a small (or in some cases large) number of institutions band together to pool limited resources and to encourage dialogue between faculty members at their respective institutions. Buhl (1979), who recounts the history of a variety of consortium models, sees them functioning "primarily as catalytic agents for renewal. They stimulate useful reactions within and among institutions, reactions that will lead to healthier functioning for the achievement of educational goals" (p. 210).

Typically, an instructional development professional is hired by the consortium members or by the agency (perhaps a state department of higher education) wishing to instigate the instructional improvement activities. Operating from a home base (at one of the institutions or at some independent or administrative location), the instructional developer allocates a certain percentage of time to each of the different institutions. Her or his activities may include consulting with individual faculty members, discussing proposed curricular revisions with departments, and serving as mentor to new faculty members. In addition, the developer arranges a series of public activities, frequently workshops, seminars, or the like, for faculty from all or several of the participating institutions.

Buhl (1979) considers a variety of theoretical as well as practical concerns related to the consortium model. His knowledge derives from firsthand experience with several different consortium variations. Scholl (1980) reports on instructional development experiences with the Great Lakes College Association (GLCA), a consortium of twelve independent, undergraduate, liberal arts colleges in Ohio, Michigan, and Indiana. Instructional development activities began in this already existing consortium with the formation of a task force on teaching improvement. This faculty task force received foundation support that helped launch an ambitious program of activities and opportunities that joined faculty members from all twelve institutions in the common pursuit of instructional excellence. Scholl directed these activities for a number of years and provides a remarkably candid assessment of how well the consortium model worked for this group of colleges.

Individual-based options do have potential as instructional structures. More of that potential is likely to be realized when they are used with creativity and commitment. Although meager resources can limit the effect of instructional development activities, bonafide institutional commitment goes a long way in overcoming budgetary restrictions.

The Committee Option. As already noted, in the Erickson (1986) survey, 62 percent of those responding indicated that some sort of faculty development committee existed on their campuses. This makes the committee approach a very common one, but most of the committees function in advisory capacities. Only 14 percent of them in the Erickson (1986) survey coordinated or provided services. Committees and administrators shared responsibilities at an additional 4 percent of the schools. Although advisory activities do make important contributions to improvement efforts (a matter to be discussed subsequently), the focus here is on instructional development models in which committees provide the services.

Several factors determine the success of these (generally faculty) committees in unlocking doors to better teaching. First, the committee must be empowered. It must be able to make decisions, implement plans, and pay for and evaluate them. If everything the group proposes to do must be approved by an administrator who controls the purse strings or must be passed by the faculty senate to whom the committee reports, few activities will occur. Second, the group must have time to plan and implement activities. Many faculty at many institutions already fulfill multiple committee obligations, and assignment to a committee with the catchall mandate of improving instruction at the institution may cause even the interested and qualified to blanch. Providing modest amounts of release time, or relieving teachers of other committee responsibilities at the same time, or allowing teachers to take no new advisees can reinforce an institution's commitment to the task assigned to the committee and greatly influence its productivity. Third, the committee may need access to outside resources and expertise. Faculty come to the improvement of instruction with little or no experience and little or no knowledge of available resources. One institution, for example, responded to the needs of committee members by hiring (at a very modest fee) the director of instructional development at another institution simply to be available to answer questions. The committee chairperson called the consultant whenever necessary, asking for information, ideas, and/or reactions to the deliberations and decisions of the group. Finally, the makeup of the committee plays an important role. Various constituencies from throughout the university should be included, as should people recognized as good teachers and committed to the instructional enterprise. The committee also needs to be created, appointed, and convened by some force within the institution that has credibility with faculty. If committees whose tasks are considered important get organized through the faculty senate, so be it. If they get appointed by the president or academic vice-president, so be it. If they are assembled and charged by the council of academic deans, so be it. Knowledge of institutional culture can prevent mistakes and enhance the committee's credibility and effectiveness.

The committee approach has a number of advantages. It gives the instructional improvement impetus a grass-roots orientation. Faculty come to have a vested interest in outcomes. This tends to encourage participation and makes the needed "volunteer" help in actual program activities easier to obtain. Moreover, the activities, resources, and services are much more likely to be acceptable to faculty. Committee members know firsthand the instructional needs and interests of faculty at the institution. The committee experience itself, with its possibilities of attending national conferences on teaching, exposure to resources and materials about instruction, and opportunities to converse at length with colleagues, frequently has a profound effect on the teaching of those serving on the committee.

Committees do not accomplish success automatically or easily, however. Sometimes problems result from overlooking the keys to success already discussed. Sometimes problems result from the nature of a committee and how it works. Romer (1980), who recounts the experiences of a faculty development committee at St. Lawrence University, succinctly describes the committee when he refers to it as a "clumsy device." Committees move slowly, even small ones. In the case of the committee at St. Lawrence University, Romer (pp. 77, 83) reports: "It took a year and a half to accomplish anything worth mentioning." But in spite of the limitations, optimism suffuses his final conclusion: "This is our story. We began awkwardly, we planned magnificently, what we achieved was different from our plan, and somehow we managed to influence a considerable number of our colleagues."

The Program Option. How widespread is the program option? Erickson (1986) reports that 28 percent of the schools in his survey had either programs (centers, offices, or units) or a coordinator (director) of faculty development. Certainly, having a program or unit devoted to the task of improving instruction increases the number of activities, resources, and services an institution can offer its faculty. Therefore, this option has the greatest potential for improving instruction. Such potential justifies a more elaborate exploration of the structural details associated with instructional development programs.

A review of both the literature about and actual structure of operating programs quickly reveals the inherent diversity that characterizes this option. Possibilities truly abound, and evidence as to the effectiveness of one structure over another does not preclude any possibility. Although no model distinguishes itself as "best," some structures and ways of configuring, staffing, and funding instructional development programs do have potential assets and liabilities. These relative merits deserve identification and discussion as well.

Consider first the *external organization* of an instructional development unit — where it fits in the larger university structure. In what department, division, college, or administrative unit is the program placed? It makes sense to consider such a unit's external organization along with its *mission*. This book focuses on the instructional improvement objectives, but those goals are frequently combined with others in the creation and organization of units that fulfill various functions. What kinds of links exist between improving teaching and other university activities?

One of the most natural organizational locations for offices with instructional improvement missions would seem to be within the department or college of education. After all, of all the professors among us, the ones with training and knowledge about teaching are located here. Unfortunately for a number of reasons, some real, some imagined, departments or colleges of education do not always have the credibility needed to accomplish improvement objectives.

There is another and more important reason for not locating an instructional development unit in any department, division, or college. Doing so puts the unit on the ground floor, makes it susceptible to the territorial and parochial struggles that all too often characterize university politics at low or intermediate administrative levels. The position makes it very easy for faculty to shift the focus from their teaching to the issue of power and what right a unit in another department has to tell faculty in this department how to teach, especially when those in the other unit have no knowledge of the content in this discipline.

Still, successful programs have been located in departments. The key issues in deciding the propriety of such a location for a given institution involve the credibility and respect of the department or college within which the program will be located and the ability of that unit to affect change in territories outside its boundaries.

Historically, a number of instructional development programs have been located in instructional media units or audiovisual departments. Instruction certainly can be improved by incorporating more and better audiovisuals, but frequently the instructional problems are larger. This in no way demeans the valuable contributions of the media and audiovisual components of instruction. However, the potential to realize a larger impact on teaching increases to the degree that those working with faculty can respond to a variety of instructional problems and issues. Typically, people working in these units are not trained to teach, do not teach at the institution, and hence are not perceived by faculty members as being "qualified." Nevertheless, successful programs have been and are currently located in offices that provide resources and services in the media area. Two issues are key: First, what is the relationship between the instructional technology objectives and the instructional improvement goals? Are they equal, or is one subsumed in the other? Second, are staff members who are assigned instructional improvement responsibilities qualified to work with faculty?

More recently, instructional improvement programs have been located in (sometimes married to) academic assistance programs or student learning centers. The philosophy behind the merger makes sense. This is the unit where students — so why not teachers — go when they need help. Moreover, these structures encourage both faculty and students to see the teaching-learning enterprise from the other's perspective. Students learn how faculty teach, how to take notes from lectures, and how to prepare and discuss assigned readings; faculty discover something about how students learn, how to lecture in order to facilitate the note-taking process, and how to configure content in order to respond to different learning styles. The arrangement encourages all the parties involved to see the shared aspects of the educational endeavor.

Unfortunately, the merger strongly implies that instructional improvement is a remedial activity. For some faculty, it is, but not for all. Moreover, if participation in instructional improvement is voluntary (which has been strongly endorsed), how likely are faculty to "volunteer" for improvement? One might argue that if we expect that acknowledgment from students, we certainly have the right to expect it from faculty. The argument makes sense, but faculty see sizable differences between themselves and their students. In addition, structures that coordinate work with students and work with faculty have special responsibilities and challenges in preserving the confidentialities of both. Finally, people trained and experienced in working with students may not have the training and experience necessary to work with faculty.

Again, however, successful programs are currently located in and combined with academic support centers. The answers to three questions help determine the success of this structure: How can the sense of remediation be avoided or dealt with? Can the operations of the two units be separated enough to ensure the confidentiality of both students and faculty? Are personnel trained and experienced in working with students able to work with equal success when their clients are faculty?

Offices of institutional research or units coordinating test and measurement activities sometimes become homes for instructional development programs. The strong association with research activities can be an asset in research universities where teaching may not be as highly regarded. The association adds even more credibility when some of the instructional improvement activities include a research agenda—where teaching is studied as a phenomenon in its own right.

On the minus side is the frequency with which such research units (especially test and measurement ones) are assigned summative instructional evaluation responsibilities. In this event, the unit becomes the one to collect personnel data, which—as explained in Chapter Four—compromises its ability to fulfill formative functions. Faculty may be there for help, but for the wrong reasons. The key to this arrangement involves balance: balancing research and instructional activities and balancing summative data collection with formative activities.

In still other institutions, instructional development programs are structured as free-standing units tied to the central administration, most commonly to the office of the chief academic officer. The advantage of this location is the visibility and credibility it affords the program. Placing the program at the center of an institution's academic operations reinforces the importance of the institution's commitment to instructional excellence. Moreover, such a position enables the unit to rise above the politics of the department or college level. There is no question of self-serving interests or divided loyalties.

But even this structure has its potential pitfalls. If the program is too closely tied to the administrative office, how does it guarantee faculty confidentiality? What if the chief academic officer asks to see evaluation results administered to aid in the improvement process or gives department heads access to observational assessments completed by the program's staff? Even if the confidentiality is maintained, will faculty believe that it is and divulge the detailed information necessary for one to make sound recommendations as to alternatives? This can be especially troublesome if the unit is physically located in the larger administrative office. On the other hand, if the university is large and multiple programs report to the chief academic officer, how does the instructional development unit get the attention, support, and budget it needs? If the administrator in charge supports the mission, the program will thrive. If not, the program is likely to suffer.

Generally, programs tied to the central administration are successful when they are close enough to be nurtured and supported and still flexible enough to ensure their independent operation and exclusive response to the needs of their faculty constituents.

Frequently, programs that are free-standing units combine instructional development activities with faculty and professional development functions to become "full-service" centers for faculty. Not only do they offer programs and activities to develop instructional skills, but they also coordinate faculty exchange programs, process applications for sabbaticals, provide career counseling, offer retirement planning seminars, and sometimes even address personal problems, such as chemical dependency. Such faculty and professional development objectives seem to fit more naturally into this format than the others. Obviously, however, this is the most costly of the options described. It requires an assembling of professionals with varied skills, resources, and services to meet diverse needs. Yet institutions that have chosen this option consider it a worthwhile investment, which in the long run pays large dividends in terms of faculty morale, motivation, and productivity.

The external organization and mission of the instructional development program merit careful consideration. The placement of the unit and the combining of its mission with other missions influence its credibility, its ability to provide resources and services, and ultimately its capacity to change the quality of instruction at the institution.

After considering how instructional development structures can be organized in terms of their external links and associations, it makes sense to consider next their *internal organization*. In general these offices are small units, many times with no more staff than a director and some clerical support. For this reason, the discussion of internal organization does not focus on chain-of-command or organizational charting but instead considers the qualifications of the person chosen to lead such a unit and presents potential ways of using volunteer and part-time help to increase the unit's size and impact.

Because instructional and faculty development is a bona-fide field of study, it is possible to hire a professional with an educational background in the area. Such training and expertise are advantageous, especially in an institution where no previous resources or services have been offered. Moreover, the percentage of universities with an instructional and faculty development unit ensures a pool of experienced professionals as well.

It is interesting to look at the professionals currently involved in instructional and faculty development activities because they are a truly eclectic group. No one has systematically reviewed the group's credentials, but those of us in the field frequently comment on our varied backgrounds, many of which have no bearing on the requirements of our current positions. In other words, being "educated" and "trained" as an instructional developer is an asset, but in terms of current practitioners, it is not an essential requirement. Many of the practitioners in the field were at one time or are currently faculty members who have found an appropriate outlet for a long-standing interest in college teaching. Thus institutions that contemplate inaugurating activities in this area need not rule out inexperienced and otherwise seemingly unqualified faculty candidates. Interest, enthusiasm, and motivation can compensate for lack of formal training. In fact, some writers see advantages in appointing a faculty director from within the institution. According to Mathis (1979, p. 107), "The desirability of having someone from within the university who has the confidence and support of his colleagues is an important consideration in appointing the first director. Someone from within the university will know the infrastructure well enough to minimize the amount of time needed to become acclimated."

What faculty directors lack is knowledge of the instructional development field. However, published materials of various sorts exist, model programs are available for observation, and a variety of professional meetings showcase relevant research, resources, activities, programs, and interests. Moreover, most current practitioners welcome the opportunity to share experiences and ideas. The decision of whom to hire depends on a host of variables, but those reviewing credentials ought to consider candidates with many different qualifications.

As the Erickson (1986) survey results note, many institutions involve faculty advisory groups in instructional and faculty development activities. An exploration of these functions and roles merits consideration as the internal workings of an instructional development program are considered. Faculty committees can contribute to instructional development programs in four principal ways. They can (1) advise as to the policies and practices of the program, (2) participate in the offerings and activities of the program, (3) evaluate those activities and offerings, and (4) serve as teaching and program advocates throughout the institution.

When they offer advice, faculty committees make recommendations about what they think the office ought to be doing—what workshop topics are likely to interest faculty, whether new faculty might be interested in mentoring activities, whether there is a need to offer diagnostic student evaluation activities, and so on. The advice can be invaluable if those operating the unit do not teach, are in other ways removed from faculty issues and concerns, and/or need a fresh perspective on what such a unit might be doing. Committees fulfilling these functions do much to keep instructional development programs honest and on target.

Committee members may be asked to participate in activities of the office. As is always the case, this works better when the opportunity is voluntary as opposed to required. Frequently, involvement in an activity does much to energize and enthuse a faculty committee. However, those assigning committee members responsibilities must remember that in most cases faculty are not paid, rewarded, or in other ways recognized for their participation; those making the assignments must therefore be realistic about how much time and effort faculty can be expected to "volunteer." And most certainly faculty contributions need to be acknowledged and appreciated.

If committee members advise and participate, they are in a good position to evaluate program resources and activities. The purpose of the evaluation ought to be formative, that is, designed to increase the impact of what the program is attempting to accomplish. Committees find it easier to offer that kind of input if those working in the program solicit it and respond constructively to what is offered. Committees can be encouraged to take the initiative, assigning certain of their members to attend all workshops offered during a given semester, asking others to review all printed materials disseminated during the term, and encouraging still others to interview faculty who have completed a consultative association with the office. Assessments of all these activities can be offered as the committee convenes to help program staff members decide on activities and goals for the upcoming semester.

Finally, faculty instructional development committees fill certain advocacy functions. Those working in the program can advertise resources and services, but sometimes their message needs the endorsement of an objective outsider. If a committee member responds to the faculty member in the department meeting who says "nobody around here cares what we do in the classroom" by referring that person to the instructional development unit, the endorsement adds to the program's influence. Likewise, a committee member's comments in defense (or offense) of the program in the faculty senate carry more weight than comments offered by the program's director. In this way, the committee can help further the program's cause and credibility.

As already intimated, committees can and probably should fulfill more than one of these functions. All committees function more productively when they perceive their work to be valuable and significant. A committee should not be appointed merely for the sake of having one. The committee should further the objectives of the unit in real and legitimate ways.

Who should appoint the committee members? What qualifies one to serve as a member? How long should members serve? How regularly should they meet? These logistical concerns depend again on the nature of the program and the institution, as well as the functions of the committee. If committees fulfilling these kinds of functions are routinely appointed by the faculty senate, that is who should appoint this group. On the other hand, if senate committees are membered by reluctant participants, those operating the program are better advised to appoint a group of interested faculty members who are committed to the mission and purpose of the office. Successful committees have been appointed by the administrator in charge of the program, by the administrator to whom the program reports, or by the faculty members themselves. Committees should be made up of faculty members who to some degree represent the constituencies the program intends to serve. If it offers training opportunities to TAs, then TAs should be represented on the committee. If the unit works directly with new faculty, then new or relatively new faculty members should serve. If the program reaches faculty in all disciplines, then certainly the committee membership should not come disproportionately from the liberal arts. For the sake of continuity, it probably works best to rotate membership so the infusion of new perspectives is balanced with the experience and wisdom of faculty familiar with previous program operations.

The staff of a small instructional development unit can also be extended by hiring faculty members on a part-time basis. At Penn State we use a small portion of our budget to buy release time for faculty members. They may work with us half- or three-quarter-time for a semester or quarter-time throughout the year. These "faculty associates," as we call them, work with us in the day-to-day operations of the office or on a project of their or our design. To illustrate, one faculty associate interviewed some of the university's outstanding teachers and recorded and edited the interviews, adding a valuable resource to our collection. Another, interested in supporting new faculty members, organized a group of them, met with them regularly, observed them teach, and in other ways supported their instructional endeavors.

Still another recorded and edited a series of videotaped teaching samples. Another developed a set of training materials to be used by faculty meeting with other faculty members to discuss formative evaluation results. We have had no trouble negotiating with departments for release time. In fact, several department heads have seen this association as an opportunity to recognize a long-standing commitment to teaching and have even reduced the charge for release time and added to the request by releasing a faculty member from a second class at no additional charge.

"Extra" help on these terms has a number of benefits besides the low cost. It constantly infuses the program with new ideas and energy. Depending on the project, it may add to a growing collection of resources. Because faculty are independent and used to working on their own, they do not require a great deal of the kind of supervision that can burden a small office staff. Faculty members interested in teaching get an opportunity to explore their interests in completely different ways. The ones associated with our office have remarked on how the experience refreshed and rekindled their interest in teaching.

Another possibility for low-cost but effective expansion of staff can be to incorporate (on a part-time basis) recent recipients of teaching awards. In addition to the honorarium, an award could include some release time, allowing the recipient to encourage and help other instructors and to advocate instructional excellence throughout the institution. Instructional development programs can sponsor workshops in which award recipients present ideas or discuss strategies with faculty. These master teachers often make outstanding mentors. Some are also interested in preparing written resources. Having outstanding teachers associated with the operating of the instructional development unit only adds to its credibility.

Matters of funding also need to be addressed. Gustafson and Bratton (1984) solicited budget information from the sixty-seven schools in their survey but caution that the data should only be reviewed for trends. Budgets ranged from $6 million to $5,000, with a mean of $501,000 or $195,000, depending on whether the budget was the largest or smallest reported by the program. Unfortunately, these figures do not accurately reflect how much the institutions actually spent on improving instruction because some of the budgets included funding for other activities supported by the unit. For example, one program in the survey provided all audiovisual equipment and production services out of its budget. Another operated a national film and videotape rental library service.

Moreover, the survey data offer no hint of what degree of funding is adequate, appropriate, or otherwise necessary for the successful operation of an instructional development unit. Most practitioners operating programs feel underfunded, that is, that they cannot realistically accomplish the task they have been given with the funds provided. Yet even a shoestring operation can make a difference in the instructional life of an institution. One problem with chronic underfunding is that it can be taken as a continuing sign of the devaluing of instructional excellence. If teaching is important and does matter, one expects the office responsible for supporting it to look respectable, to have the resources to produce and distribute professional-looking materials, and to provide professional development opportunities for its staff members. Otherwise, what should encourage faculty to greater effort may in fact do exactly the opposite.

The best advice in regard to funding seems to be to devote whatever resources are available to the enterprise. If those resources are modest, perhaps temporary internal allocations can be made for special projects. This keeps an operation fresh and vigorous even if the regular funding remains inadequate but stable across a number of years.

External sources of funds for fairly conventional instructional development activities (for example, starting a program and offering resources and activities such as those described in this book) are scarce. Universities did better in this area in the early 1970s, when instructional and faculty development was a new idea, although even during that era, Centra (1978) reports, only 30 percent of program funding came from other than institutional general budgets. Some universities are seeking to support instructional development activities with individual gifts or as part of capital campaigns. One college, at the urging of an award-winning teacher, solicited former students of that teacher, inviting them to make a gift in honor of the faculty member, a gift that would be used to support activities to further instructional excellence throughout the institution. Now the pitch is a regular one, and the instructional development unit has for the last several years realized a 25 percent budget increase. Creative approaches like this may be more productive than tapping the highly competitive and almost dry foundation and grant well.

As for evaluating these programs or units, some (Hoyt and Howard, 1978) are critical of the anecdotal evidence most often collected to support the value of the programs and the contribution they make to the instructional development process. Of three kinds of evaluative evidence, Hoyt and Howard (p. 26) see descriptions of "how participants feel about their experiences — their satisfaction, sense of well-being, willingness to recommend the experience to others, etc." as being "the least useful type of evaluative data, largely because social pressures to be polite or say the right thing . . . may result in inaccurate interpretations." They go on to point out that the bulk of the data they found to review fell into this category. Indications from interview materials reported in Chapter Nine confirm a continuing reliance on this brand of feedback. Yet perhaps not all the blame belongs to those operating the units. A review by Dunkin (1986, p. 774) describes other essential and relevant research that is missing: "There has been little research on teaching skills in higher education, and so the efforts of faculty development agents are much in need of support from that quarter. The roles played by teachers' beliefs, values, and attitudes toward teaching and learning need to be explored in the context of teaching improvement efforts."

Thus far the different ways and means of organizing and operating instructional development units have been identified and assessed. As the details show, options abound, which may confuse and frustrate the administrator or interested faculty member who would like to initiate or improve offerings in the area. What is the right, easiest, or best place to start?

One answer is to consult additional published resources that also address the issues raised in this chapter. Several different sources deserve consideration; some offer advice. For recommendations of what to do, see Chapter Eleven in Eble and McKeachie (1985); for advice on what not to do, see Hammons and Wallace (1976). Lindquist (1979) wrote the first book on instructional improvement programs, and although many of the references to specific programs are now dated, the majority of issues associated with initiating and organizing programs are still relevant. One can also learn much from the early history of this movement. More recently, Wadsworth (1988) and two associate editors have assembled for members of the Professional and Organizational Development Network (POD) *A Handbook for New Practitioners*. This gives advice from current practitioners to people just starting activities designed to improve teaching. It covers a wide range of topics, including "low budget tips" for programming, a sample program for new faculty members, and advice on promoting programs. Menges and Mathis (1988) have assembled a collection entitled *Key Resources on Teaching, Learning, Curriculum, and Faculty Development*. Its chapter on faculty development serves to alert interested parties to still more relevant and valuable resources. The *Journal of Staff, Program, and Organization Development*, published quarterly, includes many articles of interest to those working to facilitate instructional development. For example, a recent issue contains an excellent bibliography entitled "Faculty Development Resources" (Janzow and Eison, 1988).

Institutional Culture: The Decision-Making Guide

With so many different options for the organization and operation of programmatic efforts, how do institutional decision makers determine what is right and best for a particular institution? Knowing all the options may inform the decision-making process, but to no end if some guidelines do not lead decision makers to the right options. In this case, guidance does not come from the research. No evidence documents the superior success or effectiveness of one option over another. In fact, the reality of successfully operating programs and activities documents quite the opposite. A wide variety of approaches work, even those with liabilities that would seem in theory to limit or inhibit their chances of success. The needed guidelines come from elsewhere, and it is the contention of this book that they derive from knowledge of the institution. The institutional culture is what defines each individual college and university, makes one different from others, and as a consequence makes certain instructional improvement options more appropriate than others. Just as effective instructors develop styles that reflect their unique human identity, so effective instructional development initiatives evolve and come to reflect the culture and character of the institution in which they exist.

To illustrate, suppose the institution is small and prides itself on its sense of community, its closeness, its collegiality. In this environment, a highly structured instructional development program, directed by an experienced professional, hired from outside the college, who reports to the president and whose office is in the central administrative building has a much poorer chance of success than a smaller, faculty-directed office with administrative links to the faculty governance units and located among other faculty offices. Institutional culture is "usually" defined, according to Smircich (1983, p. 344), as the "social or normative glue that holds an organization together." Kuh and Whitt (1988, p. 10), in an excellent treatment of culture in colleges and universities, maintain that it serves four purposes: "(1) it conveys a sense of identity; (2) it facilitates commitment to an entity . . . other than self; (3) it enhances the stability of the group's social system; and (4) it is a sense-making device that guides and shapes behavior." In other words, a shared sense of institutional identity plays a key role in determining how we respond to new (and old, for that matter) initiatives.

The implication, then, is that those deciding how to organize and operate instructional development activities or programs must understand the culture of the institution. The assessments must be honest and candid, not the promotional images used to "sell" the institution to prospective students and donors, not pie-in-the-sky fantasies of what we wish we were or think we once were, but true answers to such questions as Who are we? What do we do? What do we value? Where do our strengths and weaknesses lie? What do our facilities say about our priorities? Which administrators have credibility and why? Which faculty have credibility and why? What are our students like? How do we teach them? Answers to these questions make instructional improvement decisions easier and more often right.

How can one determine the culture of an institution if it is unknown or unclear? Probably the most effective way is by talking to those who live and work at the institution. One can use selected interviews and/or surveys with faculty, department heads, and even students to acquire the individual perceptions needed to develop a sense of the institutional culture and its implications. If the sense of the culture is being developed to enhance instructional improvement decisions, one should ask the following specifically focused questions: What is it like to teach and learn here? How would you like to see this institution recognize and reward teaching? What should be done about teacher burnout? How satisfied are you with your teaching? In what ways could you improve it? How could the institution support your instructional efforts in and out of the classroom?

Sometimes an outside consultant, someone from another institution involved in the creation of a program or improvement initiative, can be instrumental in encouraging this sort of objective assessment and helping an institution see how its culture could be reflected in the design of instructional improvement efforts. Some institutions have charged faculty and administrative committees with preparing a report describing the instructional climate of the institution or making a series of recommendations (based on interviews and other forms of input) on how instruction at the institution might be improved given the institution's culture.

Perhaps a hypothetical example will illustrate how the culture of an institution can be reflected in the design of an institutional effort to improve instruction. Consider Currothers State University, a 10,000-student, undergraduate institution, one of eight state universities in the system. The 350 full-time faculty members, 65 percent of whom are tenured and average 48 years of age, are unionized.

Interest in instructional improvement is at the administrative level. Specifically, the vice-president for academic affairs is concerned about faculty burnout and the fact that faculty no longer seem to be responding to the instructional needs of students as well as they once did. Faculty do not share this concern; most see themselves as experienced instructors and attribute instructional problems to poorly prepared and motivated students. Faculty have standards to maintain.

The faculty-administrative relationship tends to be adversarial, primarily because of several protracted contract negotiations. However, the union is not perceived as being strong, nor is the faculty senate particularly active. Most faculty active in the union are older and not the most commonly mentioned faculty leaders. Younger faculty appear particularly disconnected from union and senate activities. On the other hand, faculty frequently describe their workload and activities in terms of their contract, using it to determine what the university can and cannot require them to do.

Faculty also feel pressured. The institution has undertaken new initiatives on several different fronts, including a major revision of general education, a review of a long-standing cooperative education program, and a preliminary proposal for an assessment program. Faculty complain about extra committee responsibilities and claim they have no time for additional activities.

Given Currothers State's institutional culture, what sort of decisions should the vice-president for academic affairs make about initiating some instructional improvement efforts? In terms of the organizational and operational details discussed, she would best be advised to consider some sort of committee approach, in spite of the faculty's committee burnout problem. The relationship between the administration and faculty rules out the option of assigning the start-up task to an administrator, and if faculty see no need for improvement, a consultant or program director is not likely to emerge from the faculty ranks. Moreover, the faculty would probably view an outside director with suspicion.

The vice-president would be well counseled to consider giving faculty members appointed to the committee a small amount of release time or at least releasing them from other committee assignments as a way of reinforcing the importance of this particular committee assignment. Unfortunately, the vice-president will probably have to appoint the committee herself because it is unlikely that the union would and would be risky if it did. She probably cannot afford to wait for the faculty senate to act on the matter. The vice-president should probably seek the advice of deans and department heads in identifying faculty receptive to the initiative. And the committee would probably do better without union representation, at least in the beginning.

As for the committee assignment, the vice-president might charge the committee with identifying what resources, services, and other kinds of institutional supports faculty think they need in order to maintain and improve the high quality of instruction they provide. As the committee seeks information and deliberates, the vice-president might underscore, for both the committee and the institution, her seriousness and commitment by providing some visible sign of her support. She could designate a facility as the future home of a teaching excellence center or arrange for a faculty classroom or meeting place to be refurbished under committee direction. She might send committee members to other institutions to view instructional supports made available to faculty elsewhere or send them to professional meetings to gather appropriate information.

The vice-president must be prepared to take the committee's recommendations seriously, to act on them even if they do not all conform to her own vision of the program. Perhaps some version of the committee should continue on into the second year, beginning the implementation of some of the recommendations. If this happens, the vice-president would be wise, given the nature of the administrative-faculty relationship, to have the committee report to some lower-level administrator. The committee also needs to be given budgetary discretion. In other words, the administrator pays the bills but lets the faculty committee set the directions so long as it can justify the expenditures as legitimate means of supporting faculty efforts in the classroom.

Given the culture of this institution, with the faculty's lack of interest or trust in improvement initiatives, the administrator should probably start small and move forward gradually. Even if the committee needs and receives some clerical support as it begins to inaugurate activities, the size and scope of the operation should be kept small. Certainly participation in all its activities should be voluntary, and no one should expect much faculty involvement in the beginning. Rather, the early emphasis must be on making every faculty involvement a positive one.

The committee should keep detailed accounts of its activities, records of its meetings, and descriptions of its discussions. These need to be combined into some sort of annual report that becomes a history of the program's development and also emphasizes next steps. The entire operation might benefit from the formative involvement of an outside consultant who reviews operations and also proposes next steps. The consultant's review must be open, shared with the committee and the administrator.

Integrating programmatic efforts into Currothers' culture will take time, perseverance, and a willingness to be satisfied with small steps forward. Clearly, this institution's faculty members will not respond favorably to having initiatives foisted on them and do not seem likely to raise issues on their own. At this institution, the interested administrator needs to cultivate the soil, plant the seeds, and carefully nurture whatever interest starts to grow.

Summary

The improvement of instruction is a complicated task for institutions and the individuals to whom it is ultimately assigned. This chapter offers a place to begin, a sense of possibilities, and an overview of various directions. The foundation laid here may offer those interested in improving instruction a solid base on which to build the kind of structure best suited to the culture of the institution involved. The program portraits in Chapter Nine further clarify the options and show how they evolve into structures uniquely suited to the needs and culture of the particular institution.

◆◆◆◆◆◆◆◆◆◆◆◆◆◆◆◆◆◆◆◆◆◆◆◆◆◆◆◆◆

9

Profiles of
Teaching Improvement
Programs

CHAPTER EIGHT explored the possibilities; this chapter details
the specifics. A sampling of current programs is described here,
with the intent of illustrating how the various instructional development possibilities proposed have been configured into actual operating units. The portraits include a brief history of each
program, current staff size and assignments, placement in the
institution's organizational structure, activities other than instructional development assigned to the unit, current sources
of program funding, and methods by which the program is
evaluated. The detailed portraits in the text are highlighted in
Table 3. The information was collected in telephone interviews
with program personnel. The portraits have been edited for ac-
curacy by the people who were interviewed.

Approximately twenty-five interviews were conducted,
beginning with programs with which the author was familiar
and continuing with programs the initial interviewees thought
should be included in the collection. Although many of the programs described here have national reputations and all are currently operational, the intent was not to discover the "best" or
"most prestigious." Rather, the goal was to assemble a collection of programs that represent different organizational and
operational configurations and different institutional settings,
although most are at large public institutions. Although instructional development is alive and well in the private sector, to date
comparatively few *programs* operate in smaller private institu-

tions. Programs were selected for inclusion in this sample because they are unique in that they are organized and operate differently than other programs in this particular collection given their institutional setting. That is, some of the relatively large institutions in the sample have comparatively small operations (usually because of budgetary constraints). Some of the smaller institutions have larger operations by contrast. Some programs, even at large institutions, rely heavily on faculty for leadership, using a sort of grass-roots model. Other programs, even at the smaller institutions in the sample, use a professional instructional development staff.

Inclusion in this sample does not imply that these are the "right" ways to organize and operate instructional development programs. In fact, some of the programs do not follow the recommendations of Chapter Eight. What becomes obvious as one reviews the portraits is the unique ways in which the programs combine and configure the elements that have been described previously. This illustrates the fact that a program must be designed so that it "fits" the climate and culture of the particular institution. What is right for one institution would never succeed at another. The diversity represented here should not confuse the issue but rather be viewed as evidence of complexity. Decisions as to the nature of instructional improvement initiatives and activities should not be made easily or offhandedly. They need to be pondered with creativity and insight. Put another way, perusal of these portraits should not be a quest for the prototype but should lead to a continuing exploration of possibilities, this time from the perspective of the actual and specific.

Center for Teaching Effectiveness
University of Texas, Austin

At the University of Texas, Austin, the Center for Teaching Effectiveness ranks as one of the longest continuously operated centers in the country. Founded in the fall of 1973, the center opened its doors in January 1974. Staff members describe it as a "university facility to assist faculty members and teaching

Table 3. Instructional Development Program Portraits.

Program Name	Years in Operation	Staff Makeup and Constituency Served	Placement in University Structure	% of Activities Devoted to Instructional Improvement	Other Activities	Source of Funding	Method of Program Evaluation
Center for Teaching Effectiveness (U of Texas, Austin)	16	Director (three-quarter-time) 1 assoc. director 1 faculty development specialist 1 grad. asst. 1 secretary _____ 2,200 faculty 1,500 TAs	Reports to provost and vice-president of university	80	Faculty and professional development	Provost's budget	Informal self-evaluation
Center for Teaching and Learning (Southeast Missouri State U)	4	Director 3 half-time directors (tutorial program, computer lab, and writing center) 1 secretary student help _____ 400 faculty	In the library, reporting to director of the library	90	Faculty development	Hard money	Formal and informal self-evaluation

Institution		Staff	Reporting structure		Focus	Funding	Evaluation
Center for Teaching and Professional Development (Sonoma State U, Calif.)	3	Director (half-time) 1 student asst. 275 faculty	Dual reporting lines, to standing faculty senate committee and dean for faculty affairs	50	Professional development; work with department heads and faculty	Line item in university budget	Informal
Faculty Center for Teaching Excellence (Western Carolina U, N.C.)	Evolving to current structure since 1981	Director 3 faculty fellows (part-time) 350 faculty	Reports to associate vice-chancellor	100		80-90% from university general budget; 10-20% discretionary, temporary funding	None to date; plan to evaluate with research design
Office of Instructional and Management Services (U of Illinois, Urbana-Champaign)	25	50 professionals; Instructional Development Division, head 4½ academic professionals 2,500 faculty 2,500 TAs	Division head reports to director of entire unit, who reports to vice-chancellor	100% for the Instructional Development Division	Instructional media, measurement and evaluation, institutional research	Hard-line budget item; 25% to Instructional Development Division	Usage of services, self-evaluation

Table 3. Instructional Development Program Portraits, Cont'd.

Program Name	Years in Operation	Staff Makeup and Constituency Served	Placement in University Structure	% of Activities Devoted to Instructional Improvement	Other Activities	Source of Funding	Method of Program Evaluation
Faculty Teaching Excellence Program (U of Colorado, Boulder)	5	Director 1 grad. asst. (half-time) 1 faculty assoc. (part-time) 1 secretary 1,700 faculty and TAs	Reports jointly with an asst. vice-chancellor to assoc. vice-chancellor	Undetermined, but primarily instructional development	Some faculty development thrusts	Academic affairs	Self-evaluation
Center for Teaching Effectiveness (U of Delaware)	Evolving since 1972, became a center in 1986	Director (quarter-time) 2 teaching consultants 1 staff asst. 1 grad. asst. (half-time) 900 faculty 400 TAs	Reports to provost and vice-president for academic affairs	95%	Faculty development	Hard money	Survey participants, annual report, periodic outside evaluation

							Self-evaluation
Office of Teaching Effectiveness (SUNY, Buffalo)	4	Director (faculty member with no release time) 1 staff associate (three-quarter-time) 1 grad. asst. student help 3,000 faculty and TAs	Reports to assoc. provost for undergraduate education	Undetermined, but mostly instructional development to date	Mission statement proposes faculty and professional development as well	University budget	
Faculty Center for Instructional Effectiveness (Eastern Michigan U)	4	Director 1 assoc. director (quarter-time) 1 assistant to the director 1 managing editor student help 680 faculty; some part-timers and TAs	Reports to provost	100%		Provost's budget	Informal
Director of Faculty Development (Goucher College, Md.)	10	Director (one-third-time) 75 faculty	Reports to dean of college	Combination of instructional and faculty development (including research and scholarship)		Permanent budget	Informal faculty interviews; part of Middle States accreditation review

Table 3. Instructional Development Program Portraits, Cont'd.

Program Name	Years in Operation	Staff Makeup and Constituency Served	Placement in University Structure	% of Activities Devoted to Instructional Improvement	Other Activities	Source of Funding	Method of Program Evaluation
Faculty Professional Development Council (State System of Higher Education, Pa. — 14 institutions in system)	4	14 faculty members 14 administrators council coordinated by vice-chancellor for academic affairs and assoc. vice-chancellor 4,500 faculty	N/A	Undetermined, but stressed improvement of teaching in first 3 years	Scholarly activities, applied research and public service, curriculum development and revision, career development	Systemwide trust fund for professional development, matching grant from system reserves, and faculty collective bargaining agreement	Review and evaluation by outside consultant

staff in any way necessary to support quality undergraduate instruction."

The center staff includes a *director,* a faculty member (currently from the Chemical Engineering Department) who spends three-quarters of his time in the center. He attends to administrative details associated with the program's operation, handles public relations matters, assists in the organization of conferences, and represents the center on various university committees. An *associate director,* currently with a background in experimental psychology, handles the day-to-day operations of the center, consulting with individual faculty members and departments, producing materials including a newsletter, and sharing the work associated with the two major conferences the center sponsors each year. A *faculty development specialist* also works on these conferences (for faculty at the institution), additionally spending a large percentage of her time consulting with faculty, supervising the center's library and its dispersion of printed materials, and conducting workshops. A *graduate assistant* handles the center's videotaping service and debriefs TAs who have been taped. The center also has a full-time *secretary.* This staff responds to the instructional needs of 2,200 faculty, 1,500 TAs and staff members (for example, librarians) who teach.

The unit is tied administratively to the chief academic office of the institution, in this case a provost and an executive vice-president. The director and associate director report on an "as the need arises" basis to an associate provost for academic activities and keep him informed and current on center activities. The center initiates its own activities. Although it "touches base" with its central administrators, it does not request permission to conduct activities unless they involve institutional policy matters. Sometimes the central administrators offer advice, but they do not set the center's agenda. Occasionally, the administration ask the center to coordinate projects that cut across college and department boundaries, such as training for international teaching assistants.

The Center for Teaching Effectiveness is funded by hard money from the provost's budget. Roughly 4 percent of the center's budget goes for operating costs and the rest for salaries.

Approximately 80 percent of the center's activities are directed at instruction. Projects include consultation, workshops, the dissemination of instructional information, the two conferences, and a videotaping service. The remainder of the center's activities fall into the faculty and professional development arena. For example, the center offers workshops on time management, getting published, and getting promoted.

This center has not felt great pressure to evaluate itself. It does evaluate its conferences but not individual consultations with faculty or its printed materials. Staff members approach evaluation informally and find that their administrators depend on personal anecdotes from faculty in assessing the center's effectiveness.

Center for Teaching and Learning
Southeast Missouri State University

A relative newcomer, the Center for Teaching and Learning was established at Southeast Missouri State University in 1985. This unit was formed by combining existing services, creating new ones, and placing all of them within the university's academic domain. Many of the existing services were student related, including a tutorial program and the writing center. Except for periodic faculty workshops, no instructional development services were available prior to the establishment of the unit.

Units combined to form the current center included the tutorial program, coordinated by a faculty member on a half-time basis; a computer lab (located in the library, where the center is also housed), run by another faculty member in a half-time position; a writing center, with a faculty director who reports to the English department; and a faculty development center. The entire unit is under the leadership of a *director* with an educational background in experimental psychology and instructional development. The present director devotes his energies primarily to the center's teaching-related activities. He was hired from outside the university when the center was established in 1985. A full-time *secretary* and several part-time *student workers* complete this center's staff. This unit responds to the instructional needs of approximately 8,000 students and 400 full-time faculty.

Administratively, the center is part of Kent Library. At Southeast Missouri State University, the library functions as a college, with the director of the library sitting on the Council of Deans. Placing the center in this "neutral" college provided an "ideal geographic location" while enabling it to represent the instructional needs of all faculty and keeping it "a safe distance" from the evaluation of faculty. The center's director reports to the director of the library, who reports to the provost.

The center's goals are (1) to facilitate instructional improvement efforts of faculty, (2) to enhance student learning, (3) to serve as a professional development resource for all who are interested in the teaching/learning process, (4) to provide outreach activities for regional pre- and postsecondary schools, and (5) to enhance the institution's reputation for excellence at the local, regional, and national levels. The student and faculty services offered are largely independent of each other. Teaching-related activities constitute approximately 90 percent of the center's faculty-related programming, with the remainder qualifying as faculty development activities.

Building renovations for the center were initially funded by the university, which later received a large private donation to cover renovation costs. The center's operations are funded with hard money, although initially funds came from a special state allocation for new programs or the enhancement of existing ones. Institutional funds have been made available for special projects. This center, along with many others, devotes the bulk of its budget to salaries.

Even though Southeast Missouri State is concerned with administrative evaluation, centers like this one are a new concept at the university and thus have not yet been evaluated. Those associated with the center anticipate an institutional evaluation shortly. The center does evaluate its own activities, using both formal and informal means. Staff members believe that anecdotal evidence does carry weight with the administrators to whom they report.

Center for Teaching and Professional Development
Sonoma State University, California

The Center for Teaching and Professional Development at Sonoma State University grew out of the recommendations of a task force originally charged with exploring the development of some sort of resource center for faculty. The idea emerged during a faculty retreat. To help determine the design of the center, the task force interviewed people at other centers to discover what their institutions were doing. The interview experience convinced them that the most "vibrant" programs were faculty run. As a result, when this center began operation in 1986, it opened under the leadership of a faculty member (from sociology). This particular faculty member had headed the original task force.

The center's *director* responds on a half-time basis to the teaching and professional development needs of 275 faculty members. The rest of the time she assumes regular teaching assignments. Center activities include publication of a newsletter, organization of a workshop series, and "management by walking around." A lot of consultation occurs spontaneously as the director and faculty members run into each other on campus. More formal exchanges occur as well, in the office or in response to classroom visits. Consultation often results in referral to sources of assistance both on and off campus.

Instructional and professional development activities are included in the program, with an equal amount of time being spent on each. Much of the professional development work involves helping department heads with human relations and management skills. Professional development for faculty focuses on writing and publication skills, time management, interpersonal conflict resolution, stress reduction, and so on.

Reflecting the center's strong faculty orientation, its director, who receives staff support from a *student assistant,* has dual reporting lines. A standing senate committee comprised of faculty representatives from each of the schools oversees the operations of the unit. The director reports to them. The committee works to publicize and disseminate information about the center. It also helps in establishing the center's goals and hires and evaluates the director. The director also reports to the dean for faculty affairs. Both reporting lines afford the director a good deal of autonomy in determining center activities.

The center is funded as a line item, and is often able to augment the budget through special in-house grant competitions. Long-term plans are to increase staff allocation so that more than one faculty member can serve on partial appointments.

Faculty Center for Teaching Excellence
Western Carolina University, North Carolina

Western Carolina University's Faculty Center for Teaching Excellence has been in the process of evolving since 1981. In 1984 the chancellor established a task force on teaching effectiveness and gave this group a three-year charge to define effective teaching and make recommendations for improving teaching at WCU. With continuing support from the chancellor and grass-roots leadership from a cadre of faculty, the task force sponsored numerous activities designed to improve teaching while they studied professional literature on the topic.

On the basis of the task force's recommendations, a previously established instructional services unit has been expanded into a center whose three goals focus exclusively on instructional development: (1) to provide a variety of general support services for teaching; (2) to provide activities designed to improve existing perceptions, policies, and practices related to teaching; and (3) to develop an outreach program for collaborating with other institutions on teaching excellence. To accomplish these goals, the center has a full-time *director* and three *faculty fellows*. The fellows are all from the institution and each has a portion of release time to work in the center. Three-year appointments to the center are staggered, and each fellow has a specific area of responsibility: program planning, publications, and internationalizing the curriculum. The fellows are assisted by volunteers from the general faculty who serve on project planning teams, a publications review board, and a financial development panel and also act as evaluation advisers. Their extensive involvement gives faculty members a sense of ownership of the center.

Operations of the center are advised, evaluated, and publicized by a ten-member faculty steering committee, including representatives of each school within the university and chaired by an elected faculty leader. The center is primarily funded with hard money from the university's general budget. Between 10 and 20 percent of the unit's budget comes from discretionary, temporary funds. This money pays for faculty retreats, luncheons, and so on that cannot be funded from the regular state budget. The director of the center coordinates the activities of the faculty fellows and reports to an associate vice-chancellor, who meets monthly with the director.

Evaluation activities have been considered in the planning activities for the center. The intent is to complete evaluation activities with research designed to generate data that can be used to add continuity and coherence to subsequent program planning.

Office of Instructional and Management Services
University of Illinois, Urbana-Champaign

Instructional improvement services have been available at the University of Illinois, Urbana-Champaign, since 1964. Most recently the institution combined instructional resources (including separate units dealing with instructional media, measurement and evaluation, and instructional development) with an institutional research unit. This department, staffed by approximately fifty professionals, describes itself as a service agency with the dual aims of enhancing instruction and meeting the data/information needs of the institution. The division within the department assigned to instructional development activities focuses its attention on better teaching. The division provides general TA training programs and also designs tailor-made programs to fit specific department needs. In addition, staff members consult with faculty, offer videotape service to TAs and faculty, conduct workshops, and promote midsemester formative feedback. (Summative evaluation is handled by another division within the same department.)

The instructional development division has a *head,* and

four and a half additional *academic professionals.* They provide
the resources and services described above to the institution's
2,500 faculty and 2,500 TAs. The division head reports to the
director of the department, who is also an associate vice-chancellor of academic affairs. The associate vice-chancellor reports
directly to the vice-chancellor, thus putting all the units in the
department high up in the structure of this large university. According to the department director, this benefits the department
(and individual units) in terms of budget, influence, visibility,
and credibility. Funds come from a hard-line budget item, with
approximately 25 percent of the department's funding going to
the instructional enhancement division.

The department director handles evaluation of the units.
He looks at usage, talks with division heads, and seeks input
from a faculty advisory committee that responds to the activities
of the entire department. The instructional development division evaluates its own workshop activities. Evaluation is seen
as thorough and ongoing.

Faculty Teaching Excellence Program
University of Colorado, Boulder

Established in 1984, the Faculty Teaching Excellence Program at the University of Colorado, Boulder, was originally part
of the University Learning Center, one of the institution's academic support services, primarily providing support to students.
The program got its start when its current director's supplemen-
tal instruction activities for students in large introductory courses
brought her in contact with faculty. In that intermediary role
she saw the relatedness of helping students and helping faculty
to succeed in challenging instructional settings, such as large
classes.

In 1988 the program was moved from the academic support services area to the academic affairs branch of the university. It now has a full-time *director,* one half-time *graduate assistant,*
some *student* work-study support, a full-time *secretary,* and one
or more *faculty associates* per year. The program buys release time
for these faculty members, who are hired to help with the

program's day-to-day operation but primarily to complete some special project. Recent faculty associates have developed the videotape consultation components of the program and studied how department heads evaluate teaching. This year's associate is working on a classroom research project. The program's staff provides instructional service to 1,700 people (including graduate instructors) who teach at the university.

The program's recent organizational move to academic affairs has put the director in weekly contact with an assistant vice-chancellor for academic affairs. The administrator is knowledgeable about the program and offers support but respects the need of the unit to function autonomously. Jointly, the director and assistant vice-chancellor report to the associate vice-chancellor. The program also receives its funding through academic affairs and expects more funds to be forthcoming in the near future.

Those within the program view its placement on the academic side of the house favorably. Earlier, they were part of a unit whose main constituency was not faculty. The program's stated goal of improving undergraduate education through faculty development focuses it exclusively on faculty. The program's activities primarily fall under the instructional development umbrella, although there have been some faculty development thrusts in retreats sponsored for new faculty members and department heads.

The director sees evaluation and program review as having precipitated the recent organizational change. (The administrators sat down and talked with faculty about the services and their experiences in the program.) She anticipates continuing evaluation of the unit and regards letters of testimony from faculty as one viable way of documenting the value of program activities.

Center for Teaching Effectiveness
University of Delaware

The University of Delaware's Center for Teaching Effectiveness evolved slowly into its current form. In 1972 an associate provost started a newsletter and grants program for instructional improvement. At around the same time, an instructional resource unit, which offered AV support services, was formed. Two instructional development consultants were hired and placed in the instructional resource unit. In 1986 the instructional development program was combined with the grants and newsletter activities to form the Center for Teaching Effectiveness with its own offices and an independent program budget.

The center is headed by a quarter-time faculty *director,* who has been given release time and is presently serving a three-year term. The director functions as chief advocate and supporter of the program and assists in its projects and activities. Running the center on a day-to-day basis is an *assistant director/teaching consultant,* who handles the budget, office management, and other logistical details and participates in planning and implementing center activities. Also working in the unit is a full-time *teaching consultant* whose time is devoted entirely to the center's instructional support and research activities. The center also has a full-time *staff assistant,* a half-time *graduate research assistant,* and some work-study support.

The center's mission is to "advance the cause of college teaching by working in partnership with university teachers to cultivate an institutional climate in which teaching is highly valued and which promotes high quality student learning." Nearly all (95 percent) the unit's efforts are aimed at instructional development (confidential teaching consultations, workshops, TA training, classroom research, and publications), although the center is including more faculty development activities. Staff members participate in planning an ongoing program for chairpersons. The center serves 900 full-time faculty and 400 TAs.

A ten-member faculty advisory board, which includes the associate provost for instruction as an ex-officio member, offers programming ideas and feedback and reviews instructional improvement grant proposals. The director appoints the committee members, who serve two-year terms. An effort is made to represent different instructional needs and interests on the committee (female faculty, minority faculty, new faculty, experienced faculty, for example.) The director reports to the provost, who is also the vice-president for academic affairs. The relationship is relatively autonomous. All programs are evaluated regularly by means of surveys of participant response, and the center prepares an extensive annual report. Periodic outside evaluation relies on both qualitative and quantitative data on program activities.

Office of Teaching Effectiveness
State University of New York (SUNY), Buffalo

The Office of Teaching Effectiveness at SUNY, Buffalo, was established by a presidential directive in May 1985. The president initiated the directive at the request of the faculty senate. In 1986 the first director of the office was appointed. During that first year he traveled around the country gathering information on the organization of similar offices and sent a grant proposal to the Lilly Endowment requesting funding for a post-doctoral teaching fellows program.

This operation is headed by a *director,* a faculty member who serves as director in addition to his regular faculty duties. He is the principal public relations person for the office, represents the office on university committees, sets policy, and lays out office activities. The director position will rotate, although policies describing the details of the rotation have yet to be established. The day-to-day operational details and most of the actual program implementation activities are the responsibilities of a three-quarter-time professional *staff associate.* The office has one assigned *graduate assistant,* as well as several work-study students. Part-time clerical support has been provided on an interim basis and has been funded externally. The office offers instructional resources and services to approximately 3,000 full- and part-time faculty members and graduate assistants.

Administratively, the staff associate and others working in the office report to the director, who in turn reports to the associate provost for undergraduate education. Although a structure of supervision exists, the office carries out most of its activities autonomously. Summary reports are submitted to the associate provost, and the director (or staff associate, depending on schedules) attends the associate provost's weekly staff meetings, at which issues concerning all facets of undergraduate education are discussed.

The office does involve faculty committees and uses them to fulfill specific planning tasks for ongoing and special programs. For example, each year a faculty committee is assembled to plan the specifics for the new faculty development summer program. In addition, an annual teaching conference is planned with the teaching quality committee of the faculty senate.

To date, the office has focused most of its activities within the instructional development area, seeking to provide faculty with practical information that can improve their effectiveness in the classroom. However, the mission statement of the Office of Teaching Effectiveness dictates a much larger function within this university community. Office functions are to include "providing referral services for faculty and graduate teaching assistants who wish to improve their teaching; assisting in the development of teaching performance assessment instruments; sponsoring and generating external funds for research on teaching; assisting in training students to design and carry out such research; sponsoring scholarly meetings, lectures, seminars, newsletters, and workshops on all aspects of the teaching-learning process; being a source of information on teaching; and promoting cooperation among on-campus centers who are presently involved in more specific missions regarding teaching." The size of the unit and its present level of funding has limited the designing and implementation of activities in all these areas.

Since 1987, the office has been funded by the university, with costs for the Postdoctoral Teaching Fellows Program (1987–90) underwritten by a Lilly grant and the Tenured Faculty Program funded by the Professional Development Quality of Working Life Committee, New York State United University Professors. Annually, the office presents the associate provost with an "asking" budget, which includes funds needed for day-to-day operational costs as well as for programs the office hopes to sponsor. The budget is funded at a certain level, with the basic operating costs being covered but with little offered in the way of support for new programs and initiatives.

Staff members expect the administration to undertake some overall evaluation of the office in the near future. As of now, they complete their own ongoing evaluation, primarily by querying participants in programs and activities about the value and usefulness of their experiences.

Faculty Center for Instructional Effectiveness
Eastern Michigan University

The Faculty Center for Instructional Effectiveness at Eastern Michigan University was begun by a provost who has a great personal interest in improving teaching. He also saw that more effective teaching was coming to the fore politically, so he began sponsoring activities out of his own office in 1985. In 1986 he appointed a half-time director, a tenured full professor, who continues to lead this center, which aims to help faculty at EMU become better teachers.

Recently, the program acquired space of its own, having previously operated out of the director's faculty office, and its staff was expanded. The *director* is joined by a quarter-time *associate director* (also a faculty member), who shares duties with the director and serves as executive editor of a journal/magazine for enhanced teaching in higher education nationwide. The center also employs an *assistant to the director,* who is primarily responsible for the center's activity announcements and in-house newsletter. A *managing editor* is assigned tasks associated with publication of the center's journal/magazine, and there is also some student help. This team offers instructional resources and activities to approximately 680 tenure track faculty, as well as part-time faculty and a few teaching assistants.

The center regards the focus of its activities as being exclusively within the instructional development arena. Evaluation activities are handled elsewhere in the university, as are a number of other activities typically associated with faculty development. To improve instruction, the center publishes an in-house newsletter, sponsors workshops and programs, runs a grants program for faculty interested in pursuing instructional innovations, and recently acquired a journal that the staff plans to develop into a national forum for the exchange of information on teaching in higher education.

Administratively, the center is connected to the provost's office, which also supplies its budget. Generally, the center initiates its own activities and programs, which the provost reviews, offering advice and recommendations. The director reports that the provost helps those working in the center to see how their operations and interests fit into the large university scheme. Occasionally, the provost assigns certain tasks to the center, some associated with its instructional development, a few related to its editorial and publishing expertise. The center puts together its own budget, which the provost approves. Special funding from sources elsewhere in the university was used to fulfill the unit's space and equipment needs.

Since the beginning, a faculty committee has advised the center. Currently, the center is in the process of revising both the scope and function of that committee. Now faculty involvement will occur via a faculty associate model. A faculty volunteer from each of the five colleges will be appointed and will participate in both the planning and implementation of center activities and programs. The intent is to broaden the faculty base so that the center can represent a larger set of instructional interests and concerns.

Director of Faculty Development
Goucher College, Maryland

The position of Director of Faculty Development was first created at Goucher ten years ago. The idea of sponsoring activities in this area came from a faculty member, who was first appointed to and still holds this one-third release time position. The director does what she has time to do for the 75 faculty members at the institution. Over the years, her activities have included leading all kinds of workshops, both on and off campus; working with new faculty; establishing a videotaping service; and participating in the Great Lakes College Association summer workshop on course design and teaching.

The director reports to the dean of the college and is advised by a faculty committee. The committee includes six faculty members, one representing each of the faculties in the college and three elected at large, and the dean. Committee membership changes each year. In addition to advising the director and supporting faculty development activities, this committee also dispenses funds for professional development and research. The committee structure is currently being reorganized. The size of the committee will be reduced and its activities combined with those of a faculty salary committee.

At this institution, faculty development is defined broadly to include activities aimed at developing instructional excellence as well as the research and scholarship of faculty. To date, professional development, such as career counseling or retirement planning, has not been included.

Faculty development activities and research activities are jointly funded as a permanent part of the college budget. The allocation was recently increased to provide funds for faculty travel. Participants evaluate workshop activities. In the past, when the president requested a program evaluation, faculty were interviewed and asked to offer input. Activities have also been evaluated as part of a recent Middle States accreditation effort.

Faculty Professional Development Council
State System of Higher Education, Pennsylvania

The Faculty Professional Development Council grew out of a series of recommendations from a joint task force representing the State System of Higher Education in Pennsylvania and the faculty collective bargaining unit, Association of Pennsylvania State College and University Faculty (APSCUF). In October 1985 the State System Board of Governors adopted the Academic Policy on Faculty Professional Development, which calls for the establishment of a joint faculty-administrative faculty development committee at each of the fourteen universities in the system and the creation of a system council. The system's Faculty Professional Development Council is composed of one faculty member and one administrator from each of the universities.

The council's mission is broad: "to encourage continuous attention to the professional growth and development of system faculty as teaching scholars, i.e., persons whose scholarly activity, teaching, and public service continue to meet high professional standards." The council has divided itself into five subcouncils, each of which assumes responsibility for a specific area of faculty development: scholarly activities, applied research and public service, improvement of teaching and learning, curriculum development and revision, and career development. Each subcouncil brings to the council proposals for programs and activities. If endorsed by the council, the recommendations go to the system chancellor for final approval.

The council meets on an as-needed basis, generally four times a year. An executive committee, which includes the chairperson of each subcouncil and three members at large, develops recommendations on general policy and procedural matters for council consideration. Coordinating the activities of the council are co-chairpersons — the vice-chancellor for academic affairs and the associate vice-chancellor, approximately half of whose time is devoted to council activities.

Council members are nominated by the individual universities, with presidents nominating the administrative representative and the local union nominating faculty representatives. Council members are appointed for three-year, staggered terms. Funding for council activities originally came from a system-union trust fund earmarked for professional development and a matching grant from system reserves. The 1987 collective bargaining agreement provided additional and increased funding through the three-year contract period.

During its first three years, the council sponsored three systemwide symposiums, provided seed money for the formation of approximately twenty new disciplinary or interdisciplinary associations of system faculty, carried out a needs assessment, and contracted with two faculty members to conduct a feasibility study for a systemwide faculty internship/consultancy program. The bulk of the council's resources, however, has been devoted to an annual grants program. Each subcouncil designs one or more requests-for-proposals corresponding to its area of faculty development. These are issued as a packet to all 4,500 faculty members in the system through the fourteen university faculty development committees, which then promote, collect, and screen proposals for submission to the council.

Although the council's mission encompasses nearly all forms of professional development, it has tried to stress those areas that traditionally have received less emphasis at the university level: improvement of teaching and learning and curriculum development. All the council's symposiums have focused on issues related to curriculum or instruction; one of these, designed explicitly for members of university faculty development committees, provided models and ideas for instructional development activities at the campus level. The council recently issued a separate request-for-proposals for university special projects "intended to enhance the quality of teaching and learning at the university, and contribute to the professional development of faculty members involved and/or affected by the project." The council plans to award up to $10,000 per project funded.

With three years of activities under its belt, the council has solicited the services of an outside consultant who will review and evaluate the operations of the council to date. The intent of this review is to document and describe the impact of the council's activities so far.

Learning More About Instructional
Development Programs

Other descriptions of instructional, professional, organizational and faculty development programs exist. Chapter authors in Lindquist (1979) assembled descriptions that appear in appendices A, B, C, and D of that work. Some of these programs are still in operation; many are not. However, the point of the review ought to be to gather still further insights into the ways and means of organizing and operating such programs. Those insights can be gleaned from programs no longer in operation or no longer organized as they once were.

What should one learn by reviewing the organization and operation of a variety of instructional development programs?

Most fundamentally, that all things are possible, in two different senses. First, organizational structures and operational details are only "right" in a very general sense. What may not work at most institutions might very well work at some institutions. Second, an entirely different set of structures and operating policies from any proposed or described here may be just as effective, especially given the culture of the institution for which it is being designed and in which it operates. The point in sharing different arrangements and alternatives is to stimulate thinking, to make known the possibilities and thereby facilitate informed decision making.

Reviewing the organizational structures and operating procedures of current (and no longer current) programs can be helpful to those interested in creating new programs or contemplating revisions of existing ones, but the focus is very much on details. One needs to stand back and put the theory of Chapter Eight and the practices of Chapter Nine into some larger perspective. To provide that perspective, the people interviewed about the programs described here were asked one final question. If they could offer advice to people beginning or refocusing initiatives in the instructional development area, what advice would they offer? What is most important as one begins or renews a commitment in this area?

The answers differed, but most focused on several key issues. A number of these practicing instructional developers emphasized the importance of *beginning with the faculty*. M. Shea (interview with the author, Sept. 15, 1988), who directs the Faculty Teaching Excellence Program at the University of Colorado, Boulder, suggests that those starting a program "begin by talking with faculty. The program needs to belong to them." N. Henderson (interview with the author, Dec. 7, 1988) of the Office of Teaching Effectiveness at SUNY, Buffalo, speaks of the importance of the initiative for the unit coming from faculty. B. Ward (interview with the author, Sept. 16, 1988), who directs the Faculty Center for Teaching Effectiveness at Western Carolina University, believes program initiators must "begin by cultivating a sense of ownership by the faculty. Don't think of a center of experts trying to tell others how to teach." J. Bailey (interview with the author, Sept. 20, 1988) of the Center for Teaching Effectiveness at the University of Delaware recommends that the first activity of the unit be to find what faculty want such a unit to do and then do that. J. Jeffrey (interview with the author, May 26, 1989), who directs the faculty development effort at Goucher College, speaks of the value of having a group of faculty who have had some sort of "communal experience" and share a vision of faculty development.

Related to those answers was a second set that describe *appropriate roles for people assigned to direct activities* in this area. M. Svinicki (interview with the author, Sept. 9, 1988) of the Center for Teaching Effectiveness at the University of Texas, Austin, advises, "Trust the clients. That is, look upon your role as being a facilitator of learning, not a director of learning." J. Eison (interview with the author, Sept. 13, 1988), who directs Southeast Missouri State's Center for Teaching and Learning, recommends "engaging faculty in collaborative projects" as a way of reinforcing the shared aspects of learning about teaching. Ward compares the role of the director to that of a catalyst, one who "helps teachers teach others to teach."

While emphasizing the importance of faculty involvement and the equality that needs to characterize relations between those inside and outside the unit, these practitioners are not devaluing *the central and essential contributions the person in charge of the unit* can and should make. Eison (1988) observes, "The success of programs on so many campuses seems to reside in the talent of the director." L. A. Braskamp (interview with the author, Sept. 16, 1988), the director of the Office of Instructional and Management Services at the University of Illinois, Urbana-Champaign, comes to virtually the same conclusion: "Success of these programs is very people dependent. This means those responsible must hire people who can consult and have the interpersonal skills needed to work with faculty." C. Stasz (interview with the author, Sept. 13, 1988), director of the Center for Teaching and Professional Development and faculty member at Sonoma State, talks about "personal qualities" that enable the director to "get the trust of faculty."

The issue of *remediation and deficiency* was the focus of several answers as well. Shea advises newcomers to "present the program as one of support and not one of evaluation." Bailey recommends that programs focus on "talent development." B. Kraft (interview with the author, Dec. 15, 1988) of the Faculty Center for Instructional Effectiveness at Eastern Michigan says, "Stay away from evaluating faculty. No judging, just helping."

A number of these same practitioners offered advice on *the pace and reputation of new programs.* Svinicki advises institutions to "start small and build a solid reputation." Braskamp makes the same recommendation and proposes moving the program forward "incrementally." Eison believes it is important that new units "find ways to gain credibility for the program." He sees one of those ways as undertaking projects "that you can make happen." There is a need to be realistic about what can and cannot be accomplished given the time, resources, staff, and institutional climate. Svinicki reminds people assigned tasks in this area that "universities move with glacial speed." Henderson cautions, "Don't become discouraged" even if only a few faculty participate in some activity that has been carefully planned. If eight faculty members participate and do things differently in their classrooms the next day, a large number of students benefit.

Related to advice in the area of reputation, several instructional developers in this group talked about *the value of doing things well.* For Shea, this is a matter of being professional, "doing things in the nicest way possible." As far as Eison is concerned, this applies to everything from handouts to refreshments. "It doesn't cost that much more to go first class." The money is well spent in terms of communicating to faculty the importance and value of instructional improvement activities. Teaching has been a second-class activity for too long. Centers can do much in quiet ways to reinforce the value and recognition of teaching.

Jeffrey and Ward both speak of *the role of administrators* with interest and responsibilities related to instructional improvement. Jeffrey sees "the need to have strong administrative support." Ward offers this advice: "Open the door, create opportunities, but get out of the way and let it happen." Given the need for faculty ownership and the various ways and means of improving instruction, that seems to be particularly sanguine, summary advice.

10

♦♦♦♦♦♦♦♦♦♦♦♦♦♦♦♦♦♦♦♦♦♦♦♦♦♦♦♦

Closing Advice
on Improving
College Teaching

IN ESSENCE, what does this book say about improving college teaching? Nine conclusions and special advice to different constituencies interested in instructional improvement lie at the heart of what has been discussed here. They are summarized below although not in order of importance.

College teaching can be improved, but not easily. By its very nature, the task of improving college teaching is not easy. It is made more difficult by problems that stand in the way. The problems begin with faculty members themselves and their profession's attitudes and beliefs about teaching. But faculty are not all that stands in the way of better teaching. Institutions have created roadblocks — some by their efforts to stimulate improvement through well-intentioned but poorly conceived evaluation activities, and others by the continued devaluing of instructional excellence in their reward structures. The improvement process itself is not easy because the teaching phenomenon is far more complicated than most faculty and institutions reckon. What works well some days or in some courses or for some instructors does not work well on other days, in other courses, or for different instructors. The improvement process requires careful and continuing consideration. How should faculty members be approached? How can they be encouraged to implement the changes that need to be made? How can they be convinced to pay continuing attention to teaching? Classroom performance does not change easily, especially in significant and sustained ways.

However, the problems and complexities of instructional improvement have been acknowledged. They do exist. Their impacts are real. Nonetheless, college teaching can be improved. After clearly identifying what stands in the way of better instruction, this book proceeds to propose ways over, around, and through the obstacles. It may be that this road ought not to be traveled by the faint of heart, but there is no question that routes to better teaching do exist and can be negotiated successfully.

Moreover, *the time to make new or to reaffirm old commitments to better teaching is now.* Now, more than at any other time in recent years, attention is being focused on the importance of quality college teaching. Credible educational leaders are advocating climates and conditions conducive to instructional health and well-being. Individuals and institutions are looking at what classroom experiences contribute to student success and learning outcomes.

The time is better than it has ever been because our knowledge about teaching and learning continues to grow. Research answers to questions about instructional effectiveness exist. More is known now than ever before about what works and does not work in the classroom. Granted, not everything that needs to be known is known, but enough is known to recommend ways and means of better college teaching.

Finally, those wishing to initiate improvement efforts have the recent and reasonably well-documented history of efforts to improve via the faculty/instructional development movement. We can learn much from the successes and failures of those who have tackled this task in the recent past. The wheels have already been invented. We need now to attach them to carts and move the cause forward.

Individual efforts and improvement activities need to occur in some context, via some process. Too often they are isolated and eclectic, not part of a larger, ongoing, and sustained commitment to instructional quality. Good ideas those activities and ideas may be; successful they may be, but not in an institutional sense. To commit to them reinforces the notion that teaching and its improvement are minor matters, to be "fixed" easily with a single potion all should be willing to take. Instructors are different; instructional needs and settings are different. Activities and efforts must reflect that larger context. Otherwise an individual may improve, but overall instructional quality at an institution probably will not.

This book proposes a process that reflects the centrality of the faculty member in improvement efforts. It begins by developing instructional awareness and then challenges the faculty member to elaborate, reinforce, or rectify the instructional image with input from others. With that solid sense of instructional self, the faculty member makes choices; choices of what to change and how to change are implemented, and the process ends where it began, cultivating awareness and seeking input as to the impact of the alterations.

Closely related to the matter of context and process is the certainty that *there is no single right way to better teaching*. Many activities and approaches work. They work well to the extent that they fit the character of the individual and the culture of the institution. Helping instructors and institutions discover that fit should be the primary task of those assigned instructional improvement responsibilities. The various ways to better teaching contribute to the complexity of the improvement process, but they also allow for flexibility, for freedom of choice. That adds a certain intrigue and excitement to the process. If something does not work, one can try something else. There is challenge followed by satisfaction when the efforts finally pay off. But the process takes time and is never finished. A new course, a new class, even a new day and the variables have changed; the ingredients for success need to be modified yet another time. Effective instruction is elusive and transitory.

Moreover, *teaching is not right or wrong, good or bad, effective or ineffective in any absolute, fixed, or determined sense*. The variable nature of effective instruction does not preclude generalizations as to the basic ingredients, but it does leave open the possibility of incorporating those fundamental aspects of teaching in very different ways, ways that come to represent the individual style and nature of the teacher involved. The sense of variability implies something else as well. As Fuhrmann and Grasha (1983, p. 195) succinctly describe it: "Any classroom behavior has advantages and disadvantages for the instructor and the students."

In other words, what may be effective for some, may be ineffective for others. For this reason, few (if any) teaching behaviors are uniformly good or bad in their effect.

Institutions should work to create climates conducive to the ongoing quest for instructional quality. Many (perhaps most) of our current instructional environments do not motivate or encourage faculty to excel in the classroom. Good teaching is expected, not rewarded. Efforts to improve are the responsibility of those who "need" to improve. This volume proposes instead that institutions should expect all faculty to continue their growth and development as teachers *and* should provide the resources and services necessary to support those faculty efforts. Supporting their efforts is an essential part of creating a climate for instructional excellence. Finally, faculty who demonstrate such ongoing commitment and successfully reach levels of instructional effectiveness should be rewarded.

Another closely related conclusion is that *efforts to improve should not be based on premises of remediation and deficiency.* Yes, some faculty need to improve. Almost everyone at an institution can point them out, but to do so compromises the character and integrity of improvement activities. Association with efforts to improve then carries negative connotations for everyone, whereas improvement ought to be an institutional expectation for all faculty. All faculty can teach more effectively; most should. Approaching instructional quality positively effectively empowers faculty members to pursue the objective, especially if the institution stands solidly behind their efforts.

Participation in activities aimed at improving instructional competence should be the exclusive responsibility of the faculty member. He or she decides what to do, when to do it, and for how long. There are implications and consequences to those decisions. If much improvement is required and little effort is expended, his or her actions will affect institutional decisions regarding that faculty member's position at the institution. However, those advocating better teaching and those working with faculty to achieve that goal must put all activities associated with becoming a better teacher solidly under the egis and control of the faculty member involved. To do so recognizes a fundamental fact of instructional change. Only one person decides what teaching behaviors do and do not occur in class tomorrow and that is the person teaching the class. Instructional improvement is not something one person does unto another.

As already asserted elsewhere throughout this book, however, faculty cannot be set out on the quest for better teaching unaided. Those working with faculty to improve must recognize that the faculty member alone does the improving, but they must as well recognize the need to motivate faculty participation and the need to surround faculty efforts with the resources, services, and support necessary if the efforts are to result in better teaching. Dealing with these two conflicting forces requires sensitivity and insight. Instructional improvers have more than one ball to keep in the air. Once again the complexity of the improvement process asserts itself.

There is one final conclusion, but first some advice to each of the constituencies to whom this book is addressed. *To deans, department heads, and other academic leaders:* To you belongs responsibility for creating the climate conducive to instructional excellence. Granted, the responsibilities are not yours alone, but you are in the positions to provide the leadership. Value teaching; in deed more importantly than in word. Recognize instructional excellence. Recognize as well continuing and concerted commitment to growth as a teaching professional. Understand the ongoing nature of instructional improvement. Expect it of all faculty.

To the ad hoc faculty committee assigned to assess the instructional climate of the institution and recommend improvements: Think long and hard about the culture of the institution and the implications of that culture in terms of how best to improve instruction. Avoid the temptation to succumb to the quick and easy cure for instructional woes. Recognize the complexity and diversity of the teaching process. Recognize the complexity and diversity of the improvement process. Be satisfied with laying the foundations. Getting the institution off and running in the right direction is the most important step in the long process of affecting an institution's instructional quality.

To the new instructional developer, probably assuming a new assignment for which you have little preparation and less experience: Do not lose your own instructional roots and history. Your experience as a faculty member and teacher is the foundation on which all instructional improvement efforts with other faculty will be based. You have much to learn. Devote yourself to study, both of the teaching phenomenon and the improvement of it. Learn to respect the complexity and diversity of both. Avail yourself of the knowledge and experience of those who have worked and currently are working to improve college teaching. You will find us ready and willing to share. We ask only that you contribute what you learn to our body of knowledge and willingly help the newcomers who will follow you. Last, but not least, believe in faculty. Believe they can improve your teaching; believe they want to. But recognize that you must awaken and rekindle their fundamental commitment to the teaching-learning enterprise. Approach your task with enthusiasm and creativity. Begin by knowing that it will not be easy.

To the experienced instructional developer: We have learned much, we deserve credit, but our task is not done. We must maintain our commitment and continually work to refine our approaches. We must as well record and share what we learn. In that way, the next book to summarize the instructional and faculty development movement will be a record of our progress.

To the individual faculty member who cares about the quality of instruction at his or her institution and sometimes thinks that he or she is the only one who does: Do not despair. You can make a difference. You can continue to work on your own teaching. Read about teaching, ponder and observe. Make your efforts to improve public. Talk about your activities. Solicit the advice and insight of other faculty. Some may tell you they do not know and wonder why you care. You care because it is important and does matter. So you ask someone else. Volunteer to help newcomers. Offer them the instructional advice you wish someone had given you. Engage students in your efforts to create a classroom climate conducive to learning. Yes, you are only lighting one candle, but in the darkness, one candle sheds a great deal of light.

   Better teaching is worth the effort. First to benefit from better teaching are the students. But faculty benefit too. They experience the pleasure of a job well done, and few professions offer the rich personal satisfaction teaching affords. Institutions benefit. They gain credibility and, one would hope, some day soon, prestige. Instructional excellence is as difficult to cultivate as research excellence. Institutions that do achieve it deserve recognition. And ultimately, though certainly not immediately, society benefits. Better teaching results in better learning, and the need for a thinking, reasonable, informed, and educated citizenry has never been greater.

RESOURCE A

◆◆◆◆◆◆◆◆◆◆◆◆◆◆◆◆◆◆◆◆◆◆◆◆◆◆◆◆◆◆

How Do You Teach?
A Checklist
for Developing
Instructional Awareness

1. *What do you do with your hands?* Gesture? Keep them in your pockets? Hold onto the podium? Play with the chalk? Hide them so students won't see them shake?
2. *Where do you stand or sit?* Behind the podium? On the table?
3. *When do you move to a different location?* Never? At regular ten-second intervals? When you change topics? When you need to write something on the board/overhead? When you answer a student's question? At what speed do you move? Do you talk and move at the same time?
4. *Where do you move?* Back behind the podium? Out to the students? To the blackboard?
5. *Where do your eyes most often focus?* On your notes? On the board/overhead? Out the window? On a spot on the wall in the back of the classroom? On the students? Could you tell who was in class today without having taken role?
6. *What do you do when you finish one content segment and are ready to move onto the next?* Say okay? Ask if there are any student questions? Erase the board? Move to a different location? Make a verbal transition?
7. *When do you speak louder/softer?* When the point is very important? When nobody seems to understand? When nobody seems to be listening?

Note: Reprinted from Weimer, 1987c, by permission.

8. *When do you speak faster/slower?* When an idea is important and you want to emphasize it? When you are behind where you ought to be on the content? When students are asking questions you're having trouble answering?

9. *Do you laugh or smile in class?* When? How often?

10. *How do you use examples?* How often do you include them? When do you include them?

11. *How do you emphasize main points?* Write them on the board/overhead? Say them more than once? Ask the students if they understand them? Suggest ways they might be remembered?

12. *What do you do when students are inattentive?* Ignore them? Stop and ask questions? Interject an anecdote? Point out the consequences of not paying attention? Move out toward them?

13. *Do you encourage student participation?* How? Do you call on students by name? Do you grade it? Do you wait for answers? Do you verbally recognize quality contributions? Do you correct student answers? On a typical day, how much time is devoted to student talk?

14. *How do you begin/end class?* With a summary and conclusion? With a preview and a review? With a gasp and a groan? With a bang and a whimper?

RESOURCE B

◆◆◆◆◆◆◆◆◆◆◆◆◆◆◆◆◆◆◆◆◆◆◆◆◆◆◆◆◆◆◆

Guidelines for
Classroom Observation

THE FOLLOWING procedures for developing a colleague visitation program are drawn from successful programs at Indiana and other colleges and universities. Classroom observation models emphasize a three-step consultation process which includes a pre-observation conference, classroom observation, and a post-observation conference.

Pre-Observation Conference

In the pre-observation session, the colleague observer obtains information from the instructor concerning his or her class goals, students, and particular teaching style. An interview schedule provides a brief, structured way of obtaining such information and includes the following questions:

1. Briefly, what will be happening in the class I will observe?
2. What is your goal for the class? What do you hope students will gain from this session?
3. What do you expect students to be doing in class to reach stated goals?
4. What can I expect you to be doing in class? What role will you take? What teaching methods will you use?
5. What have students been asked to do to prepare for this class?
6. What was done in earlier classes to lead up to this one?

Note: Reprinted from Sorcinelli, 1986, by permission of the author.

7. Will this class be generally typical of your teaching? If not, what will be different?
8. Is there anything in particular that you would like me to focus on during the class?

Details such as the date for the classroom observation, use of a particular observation form or method, and seating arrangement for the colleague observer should also be decided by mutual agreement at this session.

Classroom Observation

Faculty and students have identified the following as characteristics of effective teaching: organization and clarity, command and communication of subject matter, teacher-student rapport, and enthusiasm. Questions listed below may help the observer identify particular skills or techniques in the classroom which illustrate the characteristics of good teaching.

Knowledge of Subject Matter

Does the instructor exhibit mastery of the content? Is the depth and breadth of material covered appropriate to the level of course and group of students? Does material covered in this class relate to the syllabus and overall goals of the course? Does the instructor emphasize a conceptual grasp of the material? Does the instructor incorporate recent developments in the discipline? Is the content presented considered important within the discipline and within related disciplines?

Organization and Clarity

Structure: Is the instructor well prepared for class? Does the instructor provide an overview of the class? Is the sequence of content covered logical? Is the instructor able to present and explain content clearly? Does the instructor provide transitions from topic to topic, make distinctions between major and minor points, periodically summarize important concepts or ideas in the lecture? Does the instructor use examples and illustrations to clarify difficult or abstract ideas?

Teaching Strategies: Are the instructor's teaching methods appropriate to the goals of the class? Is the instructor able to vary the pattern of instruction through movement gestures, voice level, tone and pace? Does or could the instructor use alternative methods such as media, discussion, lab, questioning? Is the boardwork legible and organized? If appropriate, does the instructor use students' work (writing assignments, homework problems, etc.)? [Is] the use of various teaching strategies (lecture, handouts, media) effectively integrated?

Closure: Does the instructor summarize and integrate major points of the lecture or discussion at the end of class? Are homework or reading assignments announced hurriedly?

Instructor-Student Interaction

Discussion: How is discussion initiated? Are the purpose and guidelines clear to students? Does the instructor encourage student questions?

Kinds of Questions: Are questions rhetorical or real? One at a time or multiple? Does the instructor use centering questions (to refocus students' attention), probing questions (to require students to go beyond a superficial or incomplete answer), or redirecting questions (to ask for clarification or agreement from others)?

Level of Questions: What level of questions does the instructor ask? Lower level questions generally have a "right" answer and require students to recall or list facts. Higher level questions ask students to generalize, compare, contrast or analyze information.

What is done with student questions: Are questions answered in a direct and understandable manner? Are questions received politely or enthusiastically?

What is done with student response: How long does the instructor pause for student responses (formulating answers to difficult questions takes a few minutes)? Does the instructor use verbal reinforcement? Is there a non-verbal response (smile, nod)? Is the instructor receptive to student suggestions or viewpoints contrary to his or her own?

Presentation and Enthusiasm

Does the instructor demonstrate enthusiasm for the subject? For teaching? Can the instructor's voice be easily heard? Does the teacher raise or lower voice for variety and emphasis? Is the rate of speech too fast or slow? Is the rate of speech appropriate for notetaking? Does the teacher maintain eye contact with students? Does the instructor use facial expressions, posture, or motion to sustain student interest?

Student Behavior

Survey the class on occasion and note what students are doing. What are note-taking patterns in class (do students take few notes, write down everything, write down what instructor puts on board, copy each other's notes in order to keep up with lecture)? Are students listening attentively, slumped back in desks, heads on hands? Are there behaviors that are outside of the mainstream of class activity (random conversations among students, reading of materials not relevant to class)?

Overall

What did you like most about this particular class and/or the instructor's teaching effectiveness? What specific suggestions would you make to improve this particular class and/or the instructor's teaching effectiveness? Did you learn anything in the pre- or post-observation sessions that influenced or modified your responses? Overall, how would you rate this instructor?

Post-Observation Conference

The post-observation conference is most useful if it occurs within a few days of the classroom observation, while the activities are still fresh in the minds of the teacher and colleague observer. No later than one day following the observation, the colleague should review the notes on the class. The colleague observer should then discuss the classroom observation in depth with the teacher. A series of questions with which to initiate a follow-up discussion would include:

1. In general, how did you feel the class went?
2. How did you feel about your teaching during the class?
3. Did students accomplish the goals you had planned for this class?
4. Is there anything that worked well for you in class today — that you particularly liked? Does that usually go well?
5. Is there anything that did not work well — that you disliked about the way the class went? Is that typically a problem area for you?
6. What were your teaching strengths? Did you notice anything you improved on or any personal goals you met?
7. What were your teaching problems — areas that still need improvement?
8. Do you have any suggestions or strategies for improvement?

The colleague observer can reinforce and add to the instructor's perceptions by referring to the log of class events.

An analysis and interpretation of the classroom visit, as well as of the post-observation conference, should go to the instructor. It is important that the results of observations be shared with the faculty member being evaluated. (Colleague evaluations could also go to a departmental committee or to the chair, depending upon the departmental policies for sharing such information). It is also important that any colleague observation program emphasize the positive, constructive feature of the observation process — the improvement of instruction.

◆◆◆◆◆◆◆◆◆◆◆◆◆◆◆◆◆◆◆◆◆◆◆◆◆◆◆◆◆◆

REFERENCES

Abraham, M., and Ost, D. "Improving Teaching Through Formative Evaluation." *Journal of College Science Teaching*, 1978, 7 (4), 227–229.

Arrowsmith, W. "The Future of Teaching." In C.B.T. Lee (ed.), *Improving College Teaching*. Washington, D.C.: American Council on Education, 1967.

Association of American Colleges. *Integrity in the College Curriculum: A Report to the Academic Community*. Washington, D.C.: Association of American Colleges, 1985.

Austin, A. E., and Gamson, Z. F. *Academic Workplace: New Demands, Heightened Tensions*. ASHE-ERIC Higher Education Research Report, no. 10. Washington, D.C.: Association for the Study of Higher Education, 1983.

Ayers, W. "Thinking About Teachers and the Curriculum." *Harvard Educational Review*, 1986, *56* (1), 49–51.

Bakker, G. R., and Lacey, P. A. "The Teaching Consultant at Earlham." In W. C. Nelsen and M. E. Siegel (eds.), *Effective Approaches to Faculty Development*. Washington, D.C.: Association of American Colleges, 1980.

Barnes, C. P. "Questioning in College Classrooms." In C. L. Ellner and C. P. Barnes (eds.), *Studies of College Teaching*. Lexington, Mass.: Lexington Books, 1983.

Barnlund, D. *Interpersonal Communication: Survey and Studies*. Boston: Houghton Mifflin, 1968.

Bennett, W. E. "Small Group Instructional Diagnosis: A Dialogic Approach to Instructional Improvement for Tenured Faculty." *Journal of Staff, Program, and Organizational Development*, 1987, 5 (3), 100–104.

Bennis, W., and Nanus, B. *Leaders: The Strategies for Taking Charge*. New York: Harper & Row, 1985.

Bergman, J. "Peer Evaluation of University Faculty." *College Student Journal,* 1980, *14* (3), 1–21.

Bergquist, W. H. "The Liberal Arts College." In J. Lindquist (ed.), *Designing Teaching Improvement Programs.* Washington, D.C.: Council for the Advancement of Small Colleges, 1979.

Bergquist, W. H., and Phillips, S. R. *A Handbook for Faculty Development.* Washington, D.C.: Council for the Advancement of Small Colleges, 1975a.

Bergquist, W. H., and Phillips, S. R. "Components of an Effective Faculty Development Program." *Journal of Higher Education,* 1975b, *46* (2), 177–211.

Blackburn, R. T., and Clark, M. J. "An Assessment of Faculty Performance: Some Correlates Between Administrator, Colleague, Student, and Self-Ratings." *Sociology of Education,* 1975, *48* (3), 327–337.

Bland, C., and Schmitz, C. "Faculty Vitality on Review: Retrospect and Prospect." *Journal of Higher Education,* 1988, *59* (2), 190–224.

Boud, D., and McDonald, R. *Educational Development Through Consultancy.* Surrey, England: Society for Research into Higher Education, 1981.

Bowen, H. R., and Schuster, J. H. *American Professor: A National Resource Imperiled.* New York: Oxford University Press, 1986.

Boyer, E. *College.* New York: Harper & Row, 1987.

Braskamp, L. A., Brandenburg, D. C., and Ory, J. C. *Evaluating Teaching Effectiveness: A Practical Guide.* Newbury Park, Calif.: Sage, 1984.

Braskamp, L. A., Ory, J. C., and Pieper, D. M. "Student Written Comments: Dimensions of Instructional Quality." *Journal of Educational Psychology,* 1981, *73* (1), 65–70.

Browne, M., and Keeley, S. "Successful Instructional Development Workshops." *College Teaching,* 1988, *36* (3), 98–101.

Buhl, L. "Professional Development in the Interinstitutional Setting." In J. Lindquist (ed.), *Designing Teaching Improvement Programs.* Washington, D.C.: Council for the Advancement of Small Colleges, 1979.

Carnegie Council on Policy Studies in Higher Education. *Three Thousand Futures: The Next Twenty Years for Higher Education.* San Francisco: Jossey-Bass, 1980.

Carnegie Foundation for the Advancement of Teaching. "The Faculty: Deeply Troubled." *Change,* 1985, *17* (1), 31–34.

Carrier, C. A. "Note-Taking Research: Implications for the Classroom." *Journal of Instructional Development,* 1983, *6* (3), 19–25.

Carrier, C. A., Dalgaard, K., and Simpson, D. "Theories of Teaching: Foci for Instructional Improvement Through Consultation." *Review of Higher Education,* 1983, *6* (3), 195–206.

Cashin, W. *Student Ratings of Teaching: A Summary of the Research.* IDEA Paper, no. 20. Manhatten: Center for Faculty Evaluation and Development, Kansas State University, Sept., 1988.

Centra, J. A. "Types of Faculty Development Programs." *Journal of Higher Education,* 1978, *49* (2), 151–162.

Centra, J. A. *Determining Faculty Effectiveness.* San Francisco: Jossey-Bass, 1979.

Chait, R., and Ford, A. *Beyond Traditional Tenure.* San Francisco: Jossey-Bass, 1982.

Chiodo, J. J. "The Effects of Exam Anxiety on Grandma's Health." *Chronicle of Higher Education,* Aug. 6, 1986, p. 68.

Cohen, P. A. "Effectiveness of Student-Rating Feedback for Improving College Instruction: A Meta-Analysis of Findings." *Research in Higher Education,* 1980, *13* (4), 321–341.

Cohen, P. A., and McKeachie, W. J. "The Role of Colleagues in the Evaluation of College Teaching." *Improving College and University Teaching,* 1980, *28* (4), 147–154.

Doyle, K. *Evaluating Teaching.* Lexington, Mass.: Lexington Books, 1983.

Drucker, P. "Teaching and Learning." In J. S. Steward (ed.), *Contemporary College Reader.* (3rd ed.) Glenview, Ill.: Scott, Foresman, 1985.

Dunkin, M. "Research on Teaching in Higher Education." In M. C. Wittrock (ed.), *Handbook of Research on Teaching* (3rd ed.). New York: Macmillan, 1986.

Eble, K., and McKeachie, W. *Improving Undergraduate Educa-*

tion Through Faculty Development. San Francisco: Jossey-Bass, 1985.

Edgerton, R. "All Roads Lead to Teaching." *AAHE Bulletin.* 1988, *40* (8), 3–8.

Eisner, E. W. "The Art and Craft of Teaching." *Educational Leadership,* 1983, *40* (4), 5–13.

Elbow, P. "One-to-One Faculty Development." In J. F. Noonan (ed.), *Learning About Teaching.* New Directions for Teaching and Learning, no. 4. San Francisco: Jossey-Bass, 1980.

Erickson, G. "A Survey of Faculty Development Practices." *To Improve the Academy,* 1986, *5,* 182–193.

Feldman, K. A. "The Superior College Teacher from the Students' View." *Research in Higher Education,* 1976, *5* (3), 243–88.

Fox, D. "Personal Theories of Teaching." *Studies in Higher Education,* 1983, *8* (2), 151–163.

Franzwa, G. "Socrates Never Had Days Like This." *Liberal Education,* 1984, *70* (3), 203–208.

Fraser, B., Treagust, D., and Dennis, N. "Development of an Instrument for Assessing Classroom Psychosocial Environment at Universities and Colleges." *Studies in Higher Education,* 1986, *11* (1), 43–54.

Frederick, P. "The Dreaded Discussion: Ten Ways to Start." *Improving College and University Teaching,* 1981, *29* (3), 109–114.

French-Lazovik, G. "Peer Review." In J. Millman (ed.), *Handbook of Teacher Evaluation.* Newbury Park, Calif.: Sage, 1981.

Fuhrmann, B., and Grasha, A. *A Practical Handbook for College Teachers.* Boston: Little, Brown, 1983.

Fuller, F. F., and Manning, B. A. "Self-Confrontation Reviewed: A Conceptualization for Video Playback in Teacher Education." *Review of Educational Research,* 1973, *43* (4), 469–528.

Gaff, J. G. *Toward Faculty Renewal.* San Francisco: Jossey-Bass, 1975.

Gaff, J. G. "Overcoming Faculty Resistance." In J. G. Gaff (ed.), *Institutional Renewal Through the Improvement of Teaching.* New Directions for Higher Education, no. 4. San Francisco: Jossey-Bass, 1978.

Gleason, M. "Ten Best on Teaching: A Bibliography of Essential Sources for Instructors." *Improving College and University Teaching,* 1984, *32* (1), 11–13.

Group for Human Development in Higher Education. *Faculty Development in a Time of Retrenchment.* Washington, D.C.: *Change Magazine,* 1974.

Gustafson, K., and Bratton, B. "Instructional Improvement Centers in Higher Education: A Status Report." *Journal of Instructional Development,* 1984, *7* (2), 2–7.

Hammons, J., and Wallace, T. "Sixteen Ways to Kill a College Faculty Development Program." *Educational Technology,* 1976, *16* (12), 16–20.

Helling, B. "Looking for Good Teaching: A Guide to Peer Observation." *Journal of Staff, Program, and Organizational Development,* 1988, *6* (4), 147–158.

Hill, N. A. "Scaling the Heights: The Teacher as Mountaineer." *Chronicle of Higher Education,* June 16, 1980, p. 48.

Holmes, S. "New Faculty Mentoring: Benefits to the Mentor." *Journal of Staff, Program, and Organizational Development,* 1988, *6* (1), 17–20.

Hoyt, D., and Howard, G. "The Evaluation of Faculty Development Programs." *Research in Higher Education,* 1978, *8* (1), 25–38.

Hyman, R. T. *Questioning in the College Classroom.* IDEA Paper, no. 7. Manhatten: Center for Faculty Evaluation and Development, Kansas State University, Aug. 1982.

Janzow, F., and Eison, J. "Faculty Development Resources." *Journal of Staff, Program, and Organization Development,* 1988, *6* (4), 184–91.

Katz, J. "Teaching Based on Knowledge of Students." In J. Katz (ed.), *Teaching as Though Students Mattered.* New Directions for Teaching and Learning, no. 21. San Francisco: Jossey-Bass, 1985.

Knapper, C. K. "A Proposal for Changing Higher Education." *Teaching Professor,* 1988, *2* (2), 1–2.

Knapper, C. K., and Cropley, A. J. *Lifelong Learning and Higher Education.* London: Croom Helm, 1985.

Knowles, M. S. *The Modern Practice of Adult Education*. Chicago: Follet, 1980.

Kogut, L. S. "Quality Circles: A Japanese Management Technique for the Classroom." *Improving College and University Teaching*, 1984, *32* (3), 123–127.

Kuh, G., and Whitt, E. *The Invisible Tapestry: Culture in American Colleges and Universities*. ASHE-ERIC Higher Education Report, no. 1. Washington, D.C.: Association for the Study of Higher Education, 1988.

Lacey, P. A. "Faculty Development and the Future of College Teaching." In R. E. Young and K. E. Eble (eds.), *College Teaching and Learning: Preparing for New Commitments*. New Directions for Teaching and Learning, no. 33. San Francisco: Jossey-Bass, 1988.

Lagowski, J. J. "Faith." *Journal of Chemical Education*, 1985, *62* (10), 821.

LaPidus, J. "Preparing Faculty: Graduate Education's Role." *AAHE Bulletin*, 1987, *39* (9, 10), 3–6.

Leder, G., Jones, P., Paget, N., and Stillwell, J. "Peer Perspectives on Teaching: A Case Study in Mathematics." *Higher Education Research and Development*, 1987, *6* (2), 185–196.

Levinson-Rose, J., and Menges, R. J. "Improving College Teaching: A Critical Review of Research." *Review of Educational Research*, 1981, *51* (3), 403–434.

Lewis, K. (ed.), and Povlacs, J. (assoc. ed.). *Face to Face: A Sourcebook of Individual Consultation Techniques for Faculty/Instructional Developers*. Stillwater, Okla.: New Forums Press, 1988.

Licata, C. *Post-Tenure Faculty Evaluation: Threat or Opportunity?* ASHE-ERIC Higher Education Report, no. 1. Washington, D.C.: Association for the Study of Higher Education, 1986.

Limerick, P. "Aloof Professors and Shy Students." In M. Shea (ed.), *On Teaching*. Boulder: Faculty Teaching Excellence Program, University of Colorado, 1987.

Lindquist, J. (ed.). *Designing Teaching Improvement Programs*. Washington, D.C.: Council for the Advancement of Small Colleges, 1979.

McCabe, R. "Elevating the Professions." *AAHE Bulletin*, 1986, *39* (1), 3–6.

McGreal, T. L. *Successful Teacher Evaluation.* Alexandria, Va.: Association for Supervision and Curriculum Development, 1983.

McInnis, N. "How to Know What to Self-Renew." In R. H. Garrison (ed.), *Implementing Innovative Instruction.* New Directions for Community Colleges, no. 5. San Francisco: Jossey-Bass, 1974.

McKeachie, W. J. *Teaching Tips.* (8th ed.) Lexington, Mass.: Heath, 1986.

McKeachie, W. J. "Can Evaluating Instruction Improve Teaching?" In L. M. Aleamoni (ed.), *Techniques for Evaluating and Improving Instruction.* New Directions for Teaching and Learning, no. 31. San Francisco: Jossey-Bass, 1987.

McMullen-Pastrick, M., and Gleason, M. "Examinations: Accentuating the Positive." *College Teaching,* 1986, *34* (4), 135–139.

McNergney, R., and Carrier, C. *Teacher Development.* New York: Macmillan, 1981.

Marsh, H. W. "Students' Evaluations of University Teaching: Dimensionality, Reliability, Validity, Potential Biases, and Utility." *Journal of Educational Psychology,* 1984, *76* (5), 707–754.

Mathis, C. "The University Center." In J. Lindquist (ed.), *Designing Teaching Improvement Programs.* Washington, D.C.: Council for the Advancement of Small Colleges, 1979.

Menges, R. J. "Colleagues as Catalysts for Change in Teaching." *To Improve the Academy,* 1987, *6,* 83–93.

Menges, R. J., and Brinko, K. T. "Effects of Student Evaluation Feedback: A Meta-Analysis of Higher Education Research." Paper presented at the meeting of the American Educational Research Association, San Francisco, Apr. 1986.

Menges, R. J., and Mathis, C. *Key Resources on Teaching, Learning, Curriculum, and Faculty Development.* San Francisco: Jossey-Bass, 1988.

Middleton, A. "Teaching Awards and Tokenism." In M. Weimer (ed.), *Teaching Professor,* 1987, *1* (8), 3–4.

Miller, R. *Developing Programs for Faculty Evaluation.* San Francisco: Jossey-Bass, 1975.

Miller, R. *Evaluating Faculty for Promotion and Tenure.* San Francisco: Jossey-Bass, 1987.

Moore, W. "Increasing Learning Among Development Education Students." In J. B. Hefferlin and O. Lenning (eds.), *Improving Educational Outcomes*. New Directions for Higher Education, no. 16. San Francisco: Jossey-Bass, 1976.

Murray, H. "Low-Inference Classroom Teaching Behaviors and Student Ratings of College Teaching Effectiveness." *Journal of Educational Psychology*, 1983, *75* (1), 138–149.

Murray, H. "Classroom Teaching Behaviors Related to College Teaching Effectiveness." In J. Donald and A. Sullivan (eds.), *Using Research to Improve Teaching*. New Directions for Teaching and Learning, no. 23. San Francisco: Jossey-Bass, 1985.

Murray, H. "Acquiring Feedback That Improves Instruction." In M. G. Weimer (ed.), *Teaching Large Classes Well*. New Directions for Teaching and Learning, no. 32. San Francisco: Jossey-Bass, 1987.

Musella, D., and Rusch, R. "Student Opinion on College Teaching." *Improving College and University Teaching*, 1968, *16* (2), 137–140.

National Institute of Education. *Involvement in Learning: Realizing the Potential of American Higher Education*. Washington, D.C.: U.S. Government Printing Office, 1984.

Overall, J. U., and Marsh, H. W. "Mid-Term Feedback from Students: Its Relationship to Instructional Improvement in Students' Cognitive and Affective Outcomes." *Journal of Educational Psychology*, 1979, *71* (6), 856–865.

Redmond, M. V., and Clark, D. J. "A Practical Approach to Improving Teaching." *AAHE Bulletin*, 1982, *1*, 9–10.

Riegle, R. "Conceptions of Faculty Development." *Educational Theory*, 1987, *37* (1), 53–59.

Rigden, J. S. "The Art of Great Science." *Phi Delta Kappan*, 1983, *64* (9), 613–617.

Roe, E., and McDonald, R. *Informed Professional Judgement: A Guide to Evaluation in Post-Secondary Education*. New York: University of Queensland Press, 1983.

Romer, A. "The Role of a Faculty Committee in Facilitating Faculty Development." In W. C. Nelsen and M. E. Siegel (eds.), *Effective Approaches to Faculty Development*. Washington, D.C.: Association of American Colleges, 1980.

Rotem, A., and Glasman, N. S. "On the Effectiveness of Students' Evaluative Feedback to University Instructors." *Review of Educational Research,* 1979, *49* (3), 497–511.

Scholl, S. "The Consortium Approach to Faculty Development: The GLCA Experience." In W. C. Nelsen and M. E. Siegel (eds.), *Effective Approaches to Faculty Development.* Washington, D.C.: Association of American Colleges, 1980.

Scriven, M. "Summative Teacher Evaluation." In J. Millman (ed.), *Handbook of Teacher Evaluation.* Newbury Park, Calif.: Sage, 1981.

Seldin, P. *Changing Practices in Faculty Evaluation.* San Francisco: Jossey-Bass, 1984.

Seldin, P. (ed.). *Coping with Faculty Stress.* New Directions for Teaching and Learning, no. 29. San Francisco: Jossey-Bass, 1987.

Sharp, G. "Acquisition of Lecturing Skills by University Teaching Assistants: Some Effects of Interest, Topic Relevance, and Viewing a Model Videotape." *American Educational Research Journal,* 1981, *18* (4), 491–502.

Sherman, T. M., and others. "The Quest for Excellence in University Teaching." *Journal of Higher Education,* 1987, *58* (1), 66–84.

Skoog, G. "Improving College Teaching Through Peer Observation." *Journal of Teacher Education,* 1980, *31* (2), 23–25.

Smircich, L. "Concepts of Culture and Organizational Analysis." *Administrative Science Quarterly,* 1983, *28,* 339–358.

Sommer, R. "Twenty Years of Teaching Evaluations: One Instructor's Experience." *Teaching of Psychology,* 1981, *8* (4), 223–226.

Sorcinelli, M. D. *Evaluation of Teaching Handbook.* Bloomington, Ind.: Dean of the Faculties Office, Indiana University, 1986.

Starling, R. "Professor as Student: The View from the Other Side." *College Teaching,* 1987, *35* (1), 3–7.

Strauss, M., and Fulwiler, T. "Interactive Writing and Learning Chemistry." *Journal of College Science Teaching,* 1987, *16* (4), 256–262.

Svinicki, M. D., and Dixon, N. M. "Kolb Model Modified for Classroom Activities." *College Teaching,* 1987, *35* (4), 141–146.

Sweeney, J., and Grasha, A. "Improving Teaching Through

Faculty Development Triads." *Educational Technology,* 1979, *19* (2), 54–57.

University of London Teaching Methods Unit. *Improving Teaching in Higher Education.* Leicester, England: University of London Teaching Methods Unit, 1976.

Wadsworth, E. (ed.). *A Handbook for New Practitioners.* Stillwater, Okla.: New Forums Press (for Professional and Organizational Development Network in Higher Education), 1988.

Weimer, M. "A Conversation Agenda: Talking to a Colleague About Teaching." *Teaching Professor,* 1987a, *1* (5), 3–4.

Weimer, M. "Course Materials Review." *Teaching Professor,* 1987b, *1* (6), 3–4.

Weimer, M. "How Do You Teach? A Checklist for Developing Instructional Awareness." *The Teaching Professor,* 1987c, *1* (2), 3.

Weimer, M. "Professors Part of the Problem?" *Teaching Professor,* 1987d, *1* (7), 3–4.

Weimer, M. "Teaching Awards: Interesting Examples." *Teaching Professor,* 1987e, *1* (8), 2.

Weimer, M. "Reading Your Way to Better Teaching." *College Teaching,* 1988, *36* (2), 48–51.

Weimer, M. "Mentoring Activities for New and Old College Teachers." *Teaching Professor,* 1989, *3* (1), 1–2.

Weimer, M., Kerns, M., and Parrett, J. *How Am I Teaching?* Madison, Wisc.: Magna Publications, 1988a.

Weimer, M., Kerns, M., and Parrett, J. "Instructional Observation: Caveats, Concerns, and Ways to Compensate." *Studies in Higher Education,* 1988b, *13* (3), 299–307.

Wotruba, T. R., and Wright, P. L. "How to Develop a Teacher-Rating Instrument: A Research Approach." *Journal of Higher Education,* 1975, *46* (6), 653–663.

Zemke, R., and Zemke, S. "30 Things We Know for Sure About Adult Learning." *Training,* 1988, *25* (8), 57–61.

INDEX

228

Grade the Exam, 79

Grants, instructional, as activity for improvement, 108–109

Grasha, A., 36, 123, 202

Great Lakes College Association (GLCA), 153, 193

Group for Human Development in Higher Education, 144

Gustafson, K., 15, 149, 165

H

Hammons, J., 168

Helling, B., 36, 67

Henderson, N., 197, 199

Higher education: climate in, 130–144; culture in, 168–173; research model for, 15–16; revenue sources declining for, 14–15

Hill, N. A., 88

Holmes, S., 124

Howard, G., 167

Hoyt, D., 167

Hyman, R. T., 87

I

IDEA Paper series, 85, 87

Illinois at Urbana-Champaign, University of, Office of Instructional and Management Services at, 177, 186–187, 198

Implementation: activities for, 82, 88–89; by faculty, 35, 40–41, 46–47

Improvement process: activities for, 82–83; analysis of, 32–49, 201–202; and assessing alterations, 35, 41–42, 47–48; background on, 32–34; case history of, 42–49; and choices about change, 35, 38–40, 46; implementation in, 35, 40–41, 46–47; information gathering in, 35, 37–38, 44–46; instructional awareness in, 34–37; steps in, 34–42; summary on, 49

Indiana, consortium in, 153

Information: colleague interpretation of, 128–129; gathering, in improvement process, 35, 37–38, 44–46

Innovation Abstracts, 85

Institution: climate of, 130–144; culture of, 168–173

Instruction. *See* Observation of instruction; Teaching

Instructional awareness: activities for, 82, 87–88, 90–91, 93–94, 107–108; checklist for, 207–208; developing, 34–37, 43–44; in mentoring, 124

Instructional development: activities for, 82–110; advice on, 200–206; barriers to, 1–49; benefits of, 206; climate for, 130–144, 202; by colleagues, 111–129; commitment to, 201; conclusion on, 19–20; difficulty of, 3–20, 200–201; elements of, 51–144; environments for, 14–16; evaluation related to, 54–58; and faculty assumptions, 3–9; faculty resistance to, 16–19, 21–31; feedback in, 53–81; institutional options for, 145–206; participation in, 21–31; process of, 32–49, 201–202; and professional characteristics, 9–13

Instructional Development Program, 86, 103

Instructional development programs: in academic support centers, 158–159, 187; activities of, 176–180, 182, 184, 191, 192–193, 194; administrator/consultant option for, 150–154; advice on, 197–199; aspects of, 147–173; background on, 147–148, 174–175; and chief academic officer tie, 159–160, 181, 187–188, 190; committee option for, 154–156, 171–173, 204; consortium model for, 153; in departments, 157; evaluation of, 163, 167, 176–180, 182, 183, 186, 187, 188, 190, 192, 194, 196; external organization of, 156–160, 176–180, 181, 183, 184–185, 186, 190–191, 193, 194; faculty advisory committees for, 154–156, 162–164, 171–173, 184, 186, 187, 189–190, 191, 193, 194; funding of, 165–167, 176–180, 181–182, 183, 185, 186, 187, 188, 191, 193, 194; goals of, 183, 185, 188, 189, 195–196; history of,